MAKING

MARRIAGE

HAPPY

MAKING MARRIAGE HAPPY

Hard-Won Wisdom from Real Couples

CLAIRE VANDE POLDER

Library of Congress Control Number: 2020921717

ISBN hardcover   9781736081921
ISBN paperback   9781736081914
ISBN ebook   9781736081907

For my husband, Barry, who makes me happy

CONTENTS

INTRODUCTION

W HY DO SOME MARRIAGES LAST while others don't?
Why are some couples happy when so many others aren't?

Are some just lucky to be blessed with chemistry that makes the relationship easy?

Or do happy couples actually *do* things that make their happiness possible?

I got married when I was thirty-nine, which is relatively late. A few people around me breathed a sigh of relief that my single years were finally over, just under the wire before I hit forty.

I remember that way back when I was in my twenties, my grandmother was already pretty worried that I wasn't married. She even went so far as to suggest that maybe my standards were too high, which struck me as both insulting and hilarious—but mostly hilarious, because I knew she just wanted the best for me and genuinely worried about the Old Maid withering on the vine.

I wasn't opposed to getting married. I just hadn't met anyone that made me think that life would be better with a husband in the mix than it was as a single person surrounded by really good friends.

Meanwhile, people my age were pairing off all over the place, year after year, creating an endless cycle of engagement parties and weddings. Some of these marriages lasted and some of them didn't (but at least the newlyweds were an appropriate age, which allowed their grandmothers to sleep at night).

By the time I found someone I did want to settle down with, I had been on the receiving end of a *lot* of well-intentioned, but rarely helpful, advice. In the years I've been married, I've thought a lot about the common wisdom that's floating around, and I think we can do better.

If "How do you make a happy marriage?" were a *Family Feud* question, then I'm guessing the number one answer would be, "It takes a lot of work."

Well yes, it does. But when you really think about it, what exactly does "work" mean in this context? Is it housework? Chores every weekend? Changing the litterbox? Operating heavy machinery?

Or is "work" referring to something more psychological, like gritting your teeth and suffering the petty annoyances of sharing a home with another person? Is it holding your tongue when you want to argue? Or accepting that you will always need to unload the dishwasher because your spouse will never, ever do it?

Other common pearls of wisdom are equally as vague, like, "Good communication is the key."

Does this mean you have to tell your spouse everything that happens when the two of you aren't together, or can you keep some information to yourself? And if you have trouble expressing your emotions, or you aren't good with conflict, does that mean your marriage is doomed to fail?

Here's another: "You have to put your spouse first."

I get it, but again, huh? That's not actually possible. I need to be first. That's just how it is. If I'm not minding the store, the windows get dirty and squirrels start nesting in the attic.

Also troubling is that if you take this one too far, it seems a good way for one partner to eventually become dominant and the other subservient. I think we want to keep an eye on that.

Now, these nuggets of marital wisdom undoubtedly all have some virtue, and I'm not trying to be obtuse about the truths these phrases actually hold. I just think pithy tips and clichés can be misleading.

I wondered if I could tap into something deeper by digging into the details of how happy couples live day-to-day. I wanted to under-

stand what these phrases, and more, mean to real people *in real life*—
the stressful, cluttered lives where we have jobs to go to, kids to pick
up from soccer practice, houses to maintain, dentists to see, parking
tickets to fight, bills to pay, birthday gifts to buy, and holiday dinners
to plan with the in-laws.

How do these maxims take on meaning in the day-to-day grind of
living?

What Do Happy Couples Do?

After wondering about the answers to these questions for years, I decided to put my professional skills to use. I've spent my career as a
nonfiction television producer and writer. My work is about asking
questions, looking for answers, and telling stories. I've interviewed
hundreds of people on subjects ranging from polar bear attacks to the
pyramids in Egypt to killers on the loose and the cops who catch them.
(Pro tip: the spouse pretty much always did it, but that's a different
kind of marriage book.)

Producers learn early on that the best interviews are the ones with
people who are really passionate about their subject matter. You know
you've struck gold when you're talking to someone who is so enthusi-
astic that it's hard to make them stop. When I started talking to happy
couples about their marriages, that's the kind of interviewee I found.

I started by interviewing friends and acquaintances, wondering if
they had anything in common.

Turns out, they did. Very different couples with disparate backgrounds and life experiences had overlapping ideas in a number of
areas. I started to hear some of the same concepts and practices over
and over.

When I was done interviewing a core group, they referred me to
other happy couples they knew, and additional referrals grew from
there.

This is not a scientific book, and it hasn't been vetted by therapists or marriage and relationship experts. That kind of book is easy to find, if it's what you're after.

And I'm certainly not a marriage expert—just ask my husband.

What this book offers is a collection of wisdom, advice, secrets, strategies, and confessions from ordinary couples who describe themselves as happily married. These people sat for long, very personal interviews because they liked talking about their relationships. More importantly, they wanted to share their experiences in the hopes that others might find them helpful.

When I began this process, I wondered how many people I should talk to. How many interviews would provide a body of information worth sharing?

I decided that years of marriage are what counts. In my opinion, if you've experienced something firsthand, that gives you the right to talk about it with some authority. I started to tally up the years each interviewee had been married and ended at *one thousand years* as a worthy yield of material.

In other words, the individuals in the interview group represent more than one thousand years of married life—in which they've collected one thousand years of wisdom.

Who Are These Happily Married People?

The interviewees are regular people who have no special training. They'd never dream of telling you how to live your life; they were just willing to describe how they live theirs.

The average couple I interviewed has been married for about twenty years. The youngest couple is in their late twenties and has been married for four years, and the oldest is in their eighties and has been married for sixty-three years.

Almost all are legally married, though a few are unmarried but in long-term, monogamous relationships.

They are a diverse group: old and young, straight and gay, from a variety of faith traditions. They represent many cultures outside the United States, including Canada, England, France, India, Japan, South Korea, Peru, Vietnam, and more.

The group includes stay-at-home moms, retirees, and professionals in a wide variety of fields, including law, sales, science, finance, construction, media, insurance, medicine, real estate, education, engineering, architecture, church ministry, and human resources.

Some individuals found happiness the second or third time around, having divorced and learned some good lessons the hard way earlier in life.

I've tried to present their thoughts free from my own beliefs and biases. To that end, most of the content of this book is lifted directly from the interviews. Text has been lightly edited for grammar and clarity. For organization and ease of reading, I've grouped conversations into chapters on various themes.

Early in the interview process, it became clear that for people to share their experiences freely, their identities would need to be protected. Couples were in danger of offending their own children, shocking their aging parents, or becoming the butt of jokes at work if certain confessions could be traced back to them.

Therefore, the identities of those interviewed for this book are being kept anonymous. Rest assured, they're probably a lot like people you know—your best friend from high school, trusted co-worker, friendly neighbor, chatty hairdresser, cool aunt, workout buddy, favorite bartender, or grandfather who always made time for you.

By revealing both the good and bad, the ups and downs of these couples' lives, my hope is that you'll get an insider's look at a variety of elements that exist in happy marriages and practical actions that keep them that way. In this context, we can better understand what people mean when they're talking about the "work of marriage," and other regularly cited wisdom.

Maybe one of the stories will make you reflect on your own relationship.

Maybe it'll spark a solution to something you've been struggling with.

Or maybe you'll find it heartening to hear someone else's story of an imperfect life tinged with occasional failure and indecision. At the very least, you'll see that even happy marriages aren't always easy, though the people in them definitely think they're worth the trouble.

And along the way, if you find a tip or two that you might want to try in your own relationship, then so much the better.

So what do these happy couples do that others don't?

What do they know that could help others?

What do they know that might help you?

Their answers are inspiring, thought provoking, and often very funny.

CHAPTER 1

···

TWO BECOMING ONE

A long marriage is two people trying to dance a duet
and two solos at the same time.
—Anne Taylor Fleming

U NITY CANDLES are popular at weddings.
This is the tradition where the bride and groom each hold a
burning candle that they use to light a new candle together, which
represents the joining of two people.

Typically, after the unity candle is lit, the bride and groom blow
their own candles out.

Extinguished! Destroyed. No more single flames, only the one
they made together.

Boy, that's final. There is a version of this ceremony where the unity candle is lit but the original two candles are kept burning. This
seems a much better representation of what happens in marriage, at
least ideally. You're adding, not taking away. You're gaining a spouse,
not extinguishing yourself.

Whatever version of the ceremony is performed, the unity candle represents the idea of two becoming one, which is a pretty vague phrase we've attached to marriage. How do two people *become one* in real life?

Obviously, you become one in a certain sense by forming a new family unit, filing a joint tax return, and perhaps sharing a surname and address. But it's more than just that.

Sharing a life means you take into account your partner's likes and dislikes, fears and phobias, passions and hobbies. You have food in your house that you might not eat yourself and clothes in the closet that aren't yours. You have to learn to live with another person's habits, idiosyncrasies, and weird private stuff.

For many people, the idea of "becoming one" also requires compromise and sacrifice. But how much should you reasonably expect to give up, and when is it okay to insist on having your own way? Is marriage an endless series of negotiations?

The happy couples I interviewed had a lot to say about what it means to them for two to become one. Much of the secret to making it work seems to lie in the cyclical effect that's created when happiness is both given and received—as spouses are strengthened by what they get, they're energized to keep on giving.

Some people choose to make sacrifices on matters both great and small for the good of their marriage.

I've compromised in that I'll never be able to have video games in the house. Some wives don't mind them, but mine does.

When my husband and I were first married and broke, we couldn't afford a lot, so we had one very new, fluffy pillow and one dead pillow the thickness of a pancake. Every time I made the bed, I would look at the fluffy pillow and give it to him because I was being a good wife.

I asked him to help me make the bed one day, and he gave me the fat pillow and took the skinny pillow. "Oh, thanks, dear," I said, "but why did you give me the good pillow?" I assumed he had given it to me as a sweet gift for all the sacrifices I'd given him. Instead, he said, "Oh, that one kills my neck. I hope you don't mind, but I've been envying the skinny pillow." We still laugh about it decades later.

My husband is risk-averse, and that has been both the rock that our marriage stands on—and the rock I'd like to bash him in the head with occasionally. He doesn't jump into things easily, whether it's changing where we live or finding a new job. Sometimes that's been incredibly comforting, like the time I thought it would be fun to start an oyster farm when we lived in Seattle. He had the good sense not to go along with that.

Half the time I'm glad I can't change him, but sometimes I feel like we wind up missing things.

My wife likes to do the same thing all the time when we go out, and I hate that. She's also very much an inside person, whereas I'm an outside person. I always know going into these outings that I don't want to do it, but I also know I'm going to wind up enjoying spending time with her. Like when she says, "Let's go to Starbucks," I never really want to, even though I want to do something with her. It's the perfect picture of a compromise: I'm willing to compromise on the location to get her into a caffeinated mood where she's talking and comfortable, and then I know we'll enjoy being with each other.

❖

I used to feel very strongly that I needed to either choose marriage or career. In my field, chemistry, I have a lot of gifts and felt like, with a lot of focus, I could be a really great chemist. But having talked to people in my field, I didn't feel like it was compatible with having a family. I needed to choose one or the other.

Marriage was very important to me, and I didn't feel like I could do justice to both my career and a marriage. And so, a big part of my deciding to get married was choosing that over being career centered. I decided that my wife was more important. That decision affected the job I took. It's affected what we've done since then, although now it doesn't feel like a sacrifice. I don't wish I'd taken the other route. And I've actually found that I can be quite a good chemist in spite of this lead weight holding me back. Just kidding. I can possibly be a *better* chemist than I'd been if I'd tried to focus solely on work, because now I have more balance.

❖

The biggest challenges and arguments my wife and I have involve agreeing on the path we want our life to take. I'm very goal oriented. My three things in life are vision, process, and execution. Visualize what you want to do, develop the perfect process to get there, and then it's pure execution. The success I've had in my life has been the result of following that basic process.

But my wife and I can never seem to get past the vision stage for our life. I think we'll have it, and then she'll change her mind. Why don't we join the Peace Corps? Why don't we go on a mission to Burma? Why don't we register for the Cordon Bleu in Paris? There are a million things we could do, and there's no reason why we can't, but we don't do them. We've agreed to work out a vision, to sketch it out and come to terms with what the next one, five, ten, twenty years will look like. It's like the Israelis and the Palestinians. We've agreed on the framework to get to a deal, but in the meantime, there will be bloodshed, trade embargoes, and rocket-propelled grenades. I prefer to think the adventure is just on hold for now.

I've been ready to move from our house for over a year now, but my husband doesn't want to move. I'd be willing to pull up roots and move to Australia for the heck of it. All my life I've never stayed in one place more than a couple of years. It's a big compromise for me not to push it, to shake up life and make it more interesting, but my husband keeps me grounded. He has a life he likes to lead, and I choose to be involved in that life because I know that makes him happy. I love him so much, and out of everything in my life, he's my foundation. I'd never throw away what I have with him for a jaunt overseas for a year.

My wife and I lived in Taiwan when we were first married, and she hated it. It got worse when we had our first baby. It was overwhelming to her to be a new mother in a foreign country. I grew up in Hong Kong and came back to the United States for school, where we met. I've never been in a situation where I couldn't make myself happy. I'm laid back, and I make friends easily, but you can only do what you're capable of. I don't expect her to force herself to be happy in a culture that's completely foreign to her. If somebody asked me how I could give that all up, the question would be, "Give up what? Having our life be miserable?" That's a no-brainer.

Vacations are important, and we sometimes get into those discussions where I might want to go to the mountains, and my wife wants to go to the beach. I don't think a good compromise is to camp out on the plains, where nobody's happy. If you say, "I want my way," then it makes for a difficult decision. But if you say, "I want you to have your way," and the other person says, "No, I want you to have yours," then I think you can eventually come to a good agreement where both of you are honored in some way.

❖

Do whatever you have to do to make your marriage work, because it's expensive when it doesn't.

What about me?
Compromise doesn't have to come at the expense of independence.

I love the freedom my wife gives me to be myself. It astounds me sometimes. I guess it's because I was married before and didn't experience this, so it can sometimes take me by surprise. I got conditioned to feel like I couldn't really be myself, so now when my wife encourages me to go do something I want to do, I sometimes think, *Is this a trick?*

When I was single, I thought I was pretty hot. I was an attorney living in the city, had lots of friends, was looking good. I thought I was so independent and strong, but I'm not sure that I was as much as I am now. I think being married has shown me I don't need to assert my independence over my husband in an obnoxious, in-your-face kind of way. It's very important to know who you are so you can respect both yourself and the other person in a marriage. You're so intertwined that you can lose yourself, so you really need to be yourself and be real.

I think it's one of the biggest fallacies of marriage to think that you'll be melded into one. It won't happen, and it's not a good thing anyway. You will always be the center of your own universe. It doesn't matter how kind you are, you'll never be able to get beyond yourself completely to become melded with someone else. Therefore, the best thing you can do is recognize that same thing in your spouse and respect his or her identity.

My partner and I don't get into each other's business. We're very independent. We met as adults, and we have different worlds and different backgrounds. I would love to share more things with him, but I know there are things we can't share because our histories are different. So, when we're together, we share what's in common.

It's very important to have your own interests. To me, if you're being less than you are, there's a problem. Being who you are isn't going to fit who the other person is all the time, but you can't compromise that. You can find ways to accommodate, however.

When I first married my husband, I never wanted to be vulnerable with him. I didn't want him ever to see me cry, be upset, or be stressed, but time has a wonderful way of easing you into who you're supposed to be. I feel better about myself now as a woman than I did when I got married at thirty-two.

My partner and I give each other a tremendous amount of space to function—not have our activities infringed upon, not have them scrutinized, not have them questioned. That, to me, is very healthy.

Before my husband and I got married, I thought it was important to tell him how I felt about everything and to make sure he knew where I stood. I didn't have that idealistic, lovey-dovey thing about getting married. I don't mean to denigrate the feeling, but I wanted a more practical partnership with somebody who saw eye to eye with me on certain things.

I don't want to be the mother in our marriage. That's not my role. I don't want to have the feeling that I'm restricting my husband from doing something. I don't want to be in a marriage where he's doing things he doesn't like doing because I told him so. He needs the freedom to do some of what he wants to do.

I have a married friend who says that she and her husband haven't spent a night apart in twenty years. I don't need that, and neither does my husband. In the beginning, I could be gone for six weeks at a time with work, so we learned how to remain entwined but physically separate for long stretches. We aren't insecure about our relationship if we're in different cities.

❖

To me, the goal of marriage is helping each other become better selves. Compromise is generally the way to go, but every once in a while, you need to get your way. Compromise too much, and you become less than yourself.

Compromise may be easier to make in a marriage after you've spent some time being single.

I have a brother who's in college, and it makes me think about how I was in college. Any girl who had wanted to marry me in college was an idiot. Basically, all guys in college know is what they want right then, which is partying, or girls, or usually both. You have to get that out of your system first and figure out the things that matter to you as a person.

It's really important for people to know what lights them up. For me, it's being outdoors and being physical and building things. You don't get an opportunity to discover that when you go from high school to college and segue right into a marriage.

When I got together with my wife, I'd been living the bachelor life, and I traveled all the time. The only thing I had to my name was a scooter and eight different backpacks for every situation you could imagine. As hard as that was to give up, I remember those nights as a bachelor thinking, *I wish I had somebody to be doing this with. I'm in this amazing place doing it all by myself.*

My husband and I both felt very lonely for a long time before being married. Some people really haven't ever been single, so they might not understand how lonely it can be. Now I appreciate being together. Even when my husband and I are having conflicts, I think it's great to have somebody there.

My parents gave it all up early and never got to do any of the things they dreamed about doing because they got married and had a family. That was common in their generation, but my wife and I got married much later. We waited to have kids until later. We've both done a bunch of things in life. Maybe we haven't accomplished all that we set out to do, but we feel reasonably good about our accomplishments to date.

Once you have a family, it's hard to do those things you always wanted to do. We have kids now, and we had them soon after we were married. My husband did a lot of traveling before we got married, so now he's not looking back and saying, "I wish I'd done that." And I had enough of a career that I don't have to think I didn't get to start one. Being a little older also helped us figure out who's in charge of what. We each knew what our passions were before we got married, so it was a really easy changeover.

Marriage should complement your life and make it better and stronger, but it won't *be* your life. I think people really need to live their lives to the fullest before they get married. If you have things you really want to do as an individual, they may be easier to do before you get married. This depends on your partner, of course, but in marriage you'll need to compromise. You're going to take on someone else's needs along with your own when you make that commitment, and sometimes your own desires will need to go on the back burner. That's just the reality of it.

You trade certain kinds of activities, enjoyment, and struggles for other kinds of activities, enjoyment, and struggles. When you're in a relationship where you no longer have to struggle with loneliness, it's easy to think, "Wouldn't it be fun if I could do everything I wanted to do and not have to worry about checking in with my wife?" There's all this stuff we'd like to do as single people that we can't as married people, but that picture isn't realistic. You can't have the benefits of being married without some of the sacrifices of being married. I think in our minds we sometimes dream about merging the best parts of being married with the best parts of being single, but that's not an actual option.

Go on, do what you want. Happy couples encourage each other's interests and hobbies.

My husband built a climbing wall in the backyard. I think it's an eyesore, but it was important to him. It wasn't a big deal to me. He can do whatever he wants.

Compromise doesn't mean that nobody's happy and everybody's in the middle. My husband is a runner, and I like to garden. Sometimes I'll say, "You go for a run, and I'll garden, and we'll find something else to do together." You don't have to water down the joy of whatever it is you're trying to do to find the perfect mutual solution. I get the idea of everybody being willing to give up something, but if we always did that, then I'd never get to garden.

My husband plays tennis, and he does it entirely without me. I think it's very important: we shouldn't have to do only those activities the other one wants to do. I know he enjoys it, it's healthy, and he can make friends that he wouldn't have otherwise. Likewise, I've played in an orchestra every Monday night for the last eleven years. When I'm there, my mind is totally immersed in the music, and there's nothing else in my brain. That's like therapy for me.

How much you need to pursue interests outside your marriage depends on personality. I get my time alone because I'm a stay-at-home mom now. My husband has hobbies but nothing that bugs me. If he were the type to watch every single football game on TV, that would drive me nuts, but he pursues gardening or reading or learning a language. I think those are all great things.

My husband and I might not encourage each other in activities that would require huge amounts of time or money, or things which would take away from our family, but I'd never discourage him from doing something just because I can't do it with him.

❖

Some of our friends think my husband and I are strange because we do things apart quite a lot. We don't feel the need to do everything together all the time. Lately I've found I can tolerate horse racing, which my husband likes. He gets what he gets out of going to the track, and there's always a nice lunch, so I'm happy.

❖

Sometimes I feel like I've compromised more than my husband has in our marriage. I got what I wanted, which is a family. I'm content with that, though sometimes I think now that I should be out doing more.

Marriage has given me the security to know I could go off and do things. If I told my husband I wanted to climb Mount Everest, he'd be completely behind me. He has many more outside interests than I do, though, so I go with the flow. Maybe that's why I feel like I've compromised more than he has. He has very strong ambitions, and that's one of the things I'm attracted to in him.

"Yes" is a magic word.

Last summer my wife decided she really needed to get away, and she wanted to go to Scottsdale. It was August, and I didn't want to go because it was like 106 degrees there. But she really wanted to go, and it was important to her, so I said "Yeah, let's go." It was expensive since it was totally unplanned, but we did it anyway.

I think you can adjust to that. Most of the guys I know would have said forget that, it's not a good business decision, we need to plan ahead and get better prices. But it was important to her, and there was also a win in it for me. Could we afford it? Yes. So, do I care? To me it wasn't about the money; it was about the bigger picture.

One of the best decisions I made in our relationship was to get along with my husband's friends, whom I call the Beatnik Boys. They're all unmarried guys in their fifties with a lot of quirks and idiosyncrasies. I could see early on that they'd always been important to my husband, and I could either fight it or go with it. I decided to accept them, and now I have a good relationship with all of them.

When my wife first asked me to go shopping for clothes with her, all I heard was, *Blah, blah, blah shopping*. But I've learned something: when your wife asks you to go shopping, consider it quality control. She really cares what I think, and I now know she'll keep wearing something because we both like it. So, go buy yourself a cup of coffee and coast along. It's like saving yourself money up front.

Learn to say yes to your partner, and don't take yourself too seriously. Make yourself agreeable to your spouse when you might normally, to any other person, say no. You don't have to do everything you did the way you did before you were married. Of course, when you have a good wife like I do, who isn't going to request things that would be terribly wrong, that makes a big difference.

We all have preconceptions about the way we're going to live our lives. Since I got married, though, I've had to change my mind about things quite a few times. You can't go through life on auto-pilot.

Sometimes you need to be prepared to jettison a decision and go in a different direction.

There have been a number of instances where I wanted to do something and my husband didn't. If I say, "It's really important to me, and I'd like you to go," then he'll go. Often, he'll say afterward that he's glad he went, or glad that I talked him into it, because he had a good time.

It takes a little maturity to know that you're not going to get exactly what you want every single day, but I also look at marriage as an adventure. Why not go on that trip and see what it's like? We've taken our kids so many places, and they bitched and moaned the whole way. Then when we came home, they said, "Can we go back again?"

This is one of the best qualities in our marriage. My wife makes a suggestion, and I'm like *Oh, okay, I'll go*, if it's something she really wants. I usually find a way to have a good time, and she does the same for me. I think people forget that philosophy. Just go try it. I've told this to many people who've complained to me about their marriages. Did you try? No. Then how do you know?

No slackers allowed.
Both partners must work
to bring happiness to the other.

Whenever there's been something that I said I wanted, my wife will say, "You know what? You deserve it." She realizes I'm working hard to make things happen, so she wants to make sure I'm rewarded for making it work. If it went the other way, if neither of us was working hard or we didn't have respect for the other, then that would cause a downward spiral.

If you find yourself keeping score about how often you have to give something up or have your mind changed, then I think that's screwed up. There are times I get my way on things, and there are times when my wife gets her way on things, but I don't keep track. If you're thinking of everything in terms of battles, winning and losing, you're probably set up for conflicts for the rest of your life. Maybe there's a certain type of person who enjoys that, but I don't.

I've seen subjugating in some unhappy marriages—where one is dominant and the other is the audience, or where one's always the mentor and one's the student, for example. That makes for a bad long-term relationship. It needs to be equal.

It would be very difficult if you were always putting your partner first and they were never doing the same for you. If you're always the giver or you're always the taker, something's out of whack. If you're always putting the other person first, they should have more of a desire to do that for you.

There is a commitment in marriage that's different from dating. When you don't have that commitment, you can compromise to a certain point, but then it becomes a burden. Once my husband and I made the commitment to spend the rest of our lives together, compromise came naturally.

I don't think compromise means sacrifice. I compromise on what I can, and my wife compromises for me on other things. If it's only going one way, that's out of balance.

If I were in a relationship where I was constantly compromising, like she was always getting new stuff and I couldn't get anything because there was no money left over, I would start to think it's not working for me, and it would go south quick. But she compromises so much for me. We're both giving, and we're both getting.

In a good relationship, partners get pleasure from making each other happy. The act of giving brings them joy.

I know that in order to have stability and peace in my life, there are little things I will have to compromise on. In order for me to have the greatest amount of daily happiness, my wife's overall happiness is very important. So, I might not care to clean something, but I know that not doing it will cause her not to be happy and give me grief. She's never a diva, and she doesn't throw rock-star tantrums, but that's part of why I do what I do for her, in the most positive way. I know that this is something I might not want to do, but I do it because it's going to make her happy.

Compromise doesn't mean I never get what I really want, because I know chances are equally as good that my husband will put me first. It's not hard at all for me to put him first. It's one of the things that makes our marriage strong. It gives me so much pleasure to please him. I really like doing things that make him happy. If you're both thinking about it from that angle, then you know you're dealing with someone who's sensitive to what's really important to you.

❖

When my husband and I were getting ready to get married, I owned property and he didn't. I said, "Let's be adults. Sixty percent of marriages don't work, and we have no notion of how long same-sex marriages last because they haven't existed until now. I've got assets, so you write down what the split ought to be, and I'll write down what I think, and then we'll compare notes." It turns out that each of us was way more generous to the other person than we imagined. He wanted to make sure I was taken care of, and I wanted to make sure he was.

The idea of putting your spouse first is like reading a book or watching a movie. For example, I've never been to war. But I can suspend myself long enough to get into a book about it and really be with a character and follow them through. I think you need to do that in marriage. It's a huge thing, maybe the number one thing, to get out of my own way long enough to get into where my husband is coming from. When you become familiar with someone, you begin to like them because you understand what's happening to them and why. Your next question, then, is, *What can I do to either ease their pain or assist their joy?* That's where your job comes in as a partner.

There are some things I do just to please my wife. If you're doing something that's displeasing, what's the advantage of doing that activity? I never married my job, and I may lose track of our neighbors in ten years, but my wife and I are going to be together. We do the things we do to preserve our relationship and our love, not to make other people happy.

Some couples reject the idea of compromise.

There can be an obligation that comes with love, but my husband and I don't feel obligated at all. We're here because we want to be.

There's a myth that's very strong, and that's that a relationship means compromise. I don't believe that's true. I'm not compromising anything, and my husband's not compromising anything.

I respect what he wants to do, and he respects what I want to do. When we have conflicts, we have no problems making adjustments, but I don't sacrifice anything for this relationship.

Complement is a better term. My partner has a daughter, for example, and it took me years to accept her as a family member, a part of my life. A lot of times it was not something I even saw that I wasn't accepting.

One day her daughter wanted to borrow one of our cars. I thought she should take her mother's car because their names are the same, and this really upset my partner. In talking with her about it, I realized that I was limiting my relationship with her daughter. The experience allowed me to broaden how I see that, and that relationship has been an enriching thing to add to my life.

Everything so far has been more of a complement, enhancement, enrichment. I just don't see why a relationship should mean compromise.

For many couples, the value of life together outweighs individual desires. What they get is greater than what they give.

I've had to make sacrifices, but it's been well worth the reward: the security, the excitement, and the closeness that I've had with my wife.

There are people who are in relationships who don't want to get married because it would cramp their style. Ultimately, that's trying to have your cake and eat it, too. You're trying to have the relationship without having the commitment to it, and that just doesn't last long-term.

You can paint a picture in your head and think that if I were free of the old ball and chain, I would have done this, that, and the other thing. *If I didn't have a husband, I would have had my hot pink-painted apartment in Manhattan, three cats, an elaborate publishing job, and an entire closet of shoes.* You can think that to yourself, but it's not real. I don't think it's honest.

My partner and I come from two worlds and cultures that are very, very different. There's a huge part of my world that I wish I could share with him. I can share that with friends and with my daughter, but not with him, and it's painful. I tried to merge those worlds more at the beginning, and once in a while I'll push a little bit. But as I'm growing older, I'm controlling this impulsivity much more. And I think it's a key thing in a relationship—a lot of it has to do with controlling your impulses. I'm not going to damage my relationship trying to push that.

You do make sacrifices when you get married. An obvious one is flirting. Flirting was fun, and you don't do that anymore. But you gain something, which is well worth the tradeoff, and that's a lifelong companion. Either you have a companion and you compromise on some things, or you choose not to have a companion. When you frame the idea that way, it's obvious to me that you're doing better with the life-long companion and that you're happier.

Chapter 2

···

THE BATTLE OF WILLS

In the early years, you fight because you don't understand each other.
In the later years, you fight because you do.

—Joan Didion

I DON'T REMEMBER being taught how to fight in high school, but I
think it would have been helpful if it had at least been offered as an
extracurricular. Lacking any instruction, many people learn to fight by
trial and error, experimenting with truly bad ways to handle conflict.

For example, the old-school shouting match. It allows for really
satisfying blind rage and name-calling, but the downside is that the
physical exertion might give you a heart attack.

Psychological torture is another popular way to fight: for example,
the silent treatment. This is where you freeze out the other person by
ignoring them when they want to talk, though it takes a little acting
skill to do well.

There's also the passive-aggressive fight, which is fun because it
allows you to be mean without going to the trouble of addressing the
real issue.

Obviously, there are better ways to handle conflict than these. So, what do fights between happily married people look like? Are they different from conflict in unhappy marriages?

Is it normal to fight, or do some couples not fight at all?

In this chapter, couples reveal what they fought about in the early days and the techniques they've learned to manage conflict as the years pass. They talk about ground rules for keeping it civil, how important it is to be "right" in an argument, and how they evaluate when, and when not, to fight.

None of the happy couples would say their relationship is always easy, but many state that life today has a lot less conflict than it did when they first started.

Couples argue, and even people in happy marriages can get really angry with each other from time to time.

In the early days of our marriage, my wife and I would go through a period of harmony that I thought was great. I thought we were getting along, communicating well, having fun, enjoying each other's company. Meanwhile, my wife viewed that as very superficial. She'd think we weren't talking, that we were skirting around all the really key issues we needed to discuss.

Eventually it would just explode. It would boil over, and I'd be looking at her like, *What the hell just happened?* When it was over, she'd say it was cathartic and she felt better, but for me, it was the exact opposite. I felt bad. I felt we'd had a failure in the relationship, that a good relationship shouldn't boil over into those big shouting matches.

My wife and I both grew up in volatile households. I remember swearing, seriously vowing that was not the way it would be when I got married. I would do anything to avoid that. The result is that I either blew up or kept things bottled up. It was one extreme or the other. It took us a long time to find the middle ground.

Of course my husband and I love each other, but we both do things that sometimes annoy the other one. Last week we went to a party, and we got there really early. And he said, "What are we doing getting here so early?" He was mad, but that's part of marriage. We just accept it. We go with it. It's not going to be happy and joyous all the time.

For the first few years we were together, my husband and I fought a lot—real shouting, real fights. I'm more reserved than he is. When I used to get upset, I would hold onto it because sometimes I didn't know what I was feeling in the moment. I wanted to figure it out on my own. On the other hand, when my husband was upset, he'd want to talk and talk about it and resolve it right then. He'd push and push, and then I'd explode.

I think fighting helps you figure each other out. If it's at the beginning of the relationship, then I say keep fighting. If it doesn't work out, then there's a reason it doesn't. But if it does work out, and you've got understanding and chemistry, then it can be amazing.

Being honest can be uncomfortable, but it can also get easier with time.

You have to talk about the things that bother you, and you should try to talk properly about things on a regular basis. Something might happen and you don't like it, but you don't have time to have the argument right then. Later you have to sit down and say, "Hey, I didn't like it when you did that."

My husband and I are very different. We have to do a lot of adjusting all the time. It's not smooth sailing because we like to do different things, and our personalities are quite different. Luckily, we have a sense of humor in common.

My husband and I are two people who absolutely hate conflict, but that doesn't mean we avoid it. I speak my mind, and my husband speaks his mind. That's not the same thing as an argument.

If anything has evolved over time, it's that I don't get as stressed out when we have fights. I really hate conflict. It used to be that when we'd fight, I'd take it personally or think something was wrong with us, and it would take me a long time until everything was right again. Now I don't take it so seriously. We take conflicts as something that's going to happen naturally. I'll do the best I can, and if I miss, then I'll say I'm sorry.

When I was growing up, my parents would say, "We've never had a fight in our married life." I wasn't supposed to disagree with my husband, because that's the way I was brought up. But then when we got married, I thought, *I'm not going to do that.* As I've gotten older, I just give my opinion, and he still loves me no matter what. I disagree much more now than when we first got married, because I know I can.

I don't complain much generally. When I was younger, I thought that for me to complain about something meant that I needed to be upset about it. Now that I've been with my husband for a few decades, I've learned that it doesn't have to be upsetting to talk about feelings. Today we discuss our complaints and what we dislike without being upset.

House rules:
some couples agree to how they will and won't behave when they fight.

There are certain lines you don't cross. You just don't say certain things because you can't take them back, like fighting dirty or calling names.

❖

We never insult each other. Never.

❖

You can talk about the way you interact with each other. You can draw a line and say, "Don't talk to me that way."

❖

I think, in the happiest marriages, you go out of your way to protect and take care of the one you love. You make good choices, even in the heat of anger. Over the years I have never called my wife a name. Yes, I've been mean and selfish and ornery, but even then, I've tried to be respectful. You can still love someone, even in anger.

❖

A good argument is not going to be pretty, but you don't have to use weapons that destroy the relationship or one another. You don't have to hit below the belt. My husband and I have both always had that editing process, knowing that we can't take some things back. That has been a saving grace repeatedly in our lives.

How you fight, and the words you choose, are really important. I have to confess that I break the rules by sometimes getting in little jabs that I regret later. Then I'm lying in bed afterward and think that I shouldn't have said something the way I said it, and I'll have to go apologize.

My husband's very good at this, to his credit. He's considerate when we're fighting, and he never says anything derogatory. That's really important to me, because it shows me that even when we're not agreeing, he loves me, values me, and cares about how I feel.

You know that classic thing about never going to bed while you're fighting? My wife and I have also learned the lesson of sleep and food. When you're laying your head on the pillow at night, that's not the time to have a conversation about anything important. We try to have those conversations after we eat dinner and at least a good half hour before we go to bed. You can't forget that there's a little toddler inside each of us, and there are three things that make toddlers cranky: when they're hungry, when they're tired, or because they just pooped their pants. And that's still pretty true for us, even at our age.

My husband and I come from two different styles of arguing, which was very hard for us to work out in the beginning. He comes from a family where you don't go to bed mad, and I come from a family where you need to sleep on it.

We've decided it's better for us to call a truce when we're angry. Then, when you wake up the next day, it's still important to say, but it won't be with the heat and the emotion. You can make your point in a much more logical fashion. It's crazy to argue when you're angry. When you're saying the same, identical thing over and over, only louder, you're going nowhere.

We don't have fights that last for days. And contrary to some advice, I've gone to bed pissed at my wife, and I'm sure she has with me. But it's never carried over. The next morning, it's fine.

We live by that verse from the Bible, "Don't let the sun go down on your anger." I can't say we've ever talked about it, but I think it was understood in our marriage. Otherwise when you wake up the next morning, it's awkward, and you're right back where you were. I can't think of a time we've ever gone to bed mad or someone said, "I'm sleeping on the couch."

My wife and I bicker, but those arguments are stress releasers. We're both the type of people who say what we're feeling in the moment. There's no going into your corner, figuring it out and coming back. There's no break. We talk about it until it's solved, and our fights usually last a few minutes. I don't think we've ever gone for more than an hour being mad, ever.

One night we were driving home from the theater, and my husband would not stop telling me how to drive. After the third time he said something, I stopped the car on the side of the road and calmly said, "Okay, these are your choices. You can be quiet and stop telling me what do to, because I know what I'm doing. Or you can get out of the car and get a cab home. Do you need some money?" At first he had this shocked look on his face, and then we both started laughing.

Early in our marriage my husband had temper tantrums. I never felt threatened physically by him, but those tantrums would frighten me.

Instead of saying something, I had a tendency to placate him, but then I realized I was letting him get away with it. I decided that he was not to do this anymore.

I told him that if he had another tantrum, then I would take a baseball bat and demolish in thirteen seconds what he had done in thirteen minutes, because I was entitled to blow steam off too, every once in a while. He looked at me and said, "Well, I think that's a very reasonable arrangement." And he never had another tantrum again, ever.

How's somebody supposed to know they're doing something wrong if you don't tell them so? In all the fury, give yourself enough room to figure out what part of your partner's behavior you might be responsible for.

Many couples have hot buttons they fight about repeatedly, sometimes known as "that same, stupid argument."

The only thing that'll break up this marriage is if my husband and I decide to play tennis on the same team.

Yesterday we were doing our taxes, and my husband said something and I talked back loudly to him. We've learned over the years that when we do our taxes, we get into arguments. There's so much pressure, and we find ourselves getting snippy about nothing. Now when I realize it's the taxes that are stressing us, I apologize right away.

My husband and I have conflicts about the fact that he does not listen. It's what I get upset about the most. Sometimes I'll be talking and he hasn't heard a word I've said, and he'll then repeat what I've said as

THE BATTLE OF WILLS

his own idea. It drives me insane. Then I get irritated and snap at him, and I become a know-it-all, and then he gets irritated. It doesn't always lead to an argument, but often it does. I haven't yet learned to let it wash off my back, but I'm working on it.

My wife and I have a consistent theme in that we both have the tendency to take the other for granted. When you get married, have kids, and get in a routine, there's a certain amount of mutual taking for granted of the other person. I may be looking for a certain amount of gratitude or recognition if I've had a hard day, and if she doesn't acknowledge it, I may feel unappreciated. I have those moments, and I know she has those moments. It's still something we struggle with, but we've brought it up so many times that we understand it now.

Just last night we had a little meltdown. We're doing a house renovation and haven't gotten the plans yet, and my husband started talking about it and said the contractor would be starting in a couple of days. I flipped out. It wasn't a normal reaction, and I got more and more hyper about it. We'd had a bad experience with renovations before, and I finally said, "It's because of what happened last time, and I just don't want that to happen again." That defused the whole thing, and I was able to stop pushing him away.

❖

The last argument my husband and I had was about how late he came home from being out somewhere, and this is a recurring thing. It's not that I don't trust him or what he's doing, but when you get to a certain age, you shouldn't be coming in at four in the morning anymore. I think maybe it's just because I can't settle until he comes home. I don't completely relax. I'd prefer that he's in by one in the morning at the latest, and then we can all go to sleep. It's not one of those things that's going to destroy a marriage, but it's something we're going to continue to argue about. It's our major area of conflict—nothing else tops that.

Having that same argument over and over can be like a wedge in a log. If you know it's already caused an issue and you're not resolving it, each time you hit that wedge harder, it's not bringing that log back together. Each time you strike it, it's going to push you further apart.

If you need to be right all the time, then you just bought a ticket to the fights.

There's that classic question: Would you rather be right, or would you rather be happy? If you asked me twenty-five years ago, I'd unhesitatingly say I'd rather be right, but that was stupid. As far as marriage goes, happy is really much smarter.

I've learned so much about myself from the conflicts I've had with my husband over the years. I used to have to win all the time, right there, with no other interpretation but that I crushed you. I got that from my dad. He leaves no room for anyone else to win, and I've never heard him apologize. I'm mostly not like that anymore. It also helps because my husband is very easy to get along with. I lucked out on that.

Early on in our relationship, my husband and I fought a lot. But after we decided we wanted to be a couple, I decided that if this is going to work, we needed to be on each other's side first, regardless of whether we agree on an issue. I began to look at my defense of my husband as a human being first, because I have his back over everything else. Not that I'd back off or stop expressing my viewpoints, but winning didn't matter anymore. What mattered is that we knew we took each other's side first in all things.

I think when a person goes overboard in focusing on independence, being the strong one, and defending their right to be right all the time, that's a big relationship killer. Not only do they have to be right, they have to let everyone know they're right, especially their spouse. Well, what does that get you? You know you're right, the other person still knows you're wrong, and now you've completely alienated yourself from everybody else around you.

I used to have a boss who always had a lot of New Age sayings that I thought were a bunch of crap. He had this one that I never understood, but I understand it now as it relates to our marriage. He'd say, "Don't make other people wrong. They can be wrong, but don't make them wrong."

My wife and I will "make each other wrong" sometimes. We'll assume someone's done something out of a bad or incorrect intention. Our reactions to our kids can be very different, for example. Sometimes we'll make a judgment that the other person was wrong, rather than that they just did something differently. So, let's not blame each other, and let's not make each other wrong. I still think some of what that guy said was hippie crazy, but I buy into that one now a little bit.

I can be bossy and pushy, but I'm very conflicted with myself about that, and I know this is a conflict for other couples, too. Sometimes my husband gives up and says he's too old to fight with me, and that's not right. I think it's important always to listen to what he has to say, even when I believe I'm right. It's hard, but I really try to listen, compromise, and give him a chance to do some things the way he wants to do them.

The younger you are, the more aggressive you might be in worrying about being right or getting your way. I can tell you now that after fifty or sixty years of marriage, you know each other pretty well. You don't press for the things you know are going to be problems. It doesn't make any difference anyway. Can you imagine how many of my dirty socks and underwear my wife has laundered? And she's still feeding me. So, am I going to argue about right and wrong? Forget it.

Zip it.
Holding your tongue can prevent unimportant arguments.

I was listening to this basketball coach talk recently about his players. He was saying that he doesn't get into a lot of arguments with them unless he has to. He feels like he has about three bullets for every player, and that's how I feel about my marriage. With my wife, I'm very careful about when I choose to use a bullet, so to speak.

My husband doesn't really criticize me, which I appreciate. The meals are pretty much my job in our home. If I make a meal that's not very good, he'll just go and get a bottle of Tabasco sauce. He won't say anything, and then I know it's bland, but he doesn't criticize.

❖

Sometimes my husband asks me to help him with his chores, but then he'll constantly correct me. Like if I'm holding a board while he's sawing, he'll say, "You need to do it this way," and he'll go through a big list of requirements. And I'll think, *Oh, my goodness.* To me it's a compromise to keep my mouth shut. This is something I've learned to deal with, and it's not that important.

It can be a problem when couples don't communicate, but we have the opposite problem sometimes. I probably over-communicate. I'll tell my husband what irritates me right away, but honestly, I don't need to talk about *everything* that irritates me. I should shut up more, and we'd probably argue less.

You can't mention every tiny thing that bugs you. If you can let it go, and in the next day or two you forget about it, then it wasn't important. Just don't let it happen too often, or you'll be seething about the fact that you keep letting things go.

I was married to my first wife at a young age, and it lasted a long time. It was a very unhappy marriage, and then I went through an extremely ugly divorce. I grew accustomed to a terrible quality of life. It's like if you grow up in Winnipeg, you think it's always 40 below in the winter, right? Well, it isn't like that everywhere.

In my current marriage, I remember in the early days my wife would say, "Oh, we're fighting." And I'd say, "Are you kidding? Holy smokes, let me tell you about fighting. This isn't fighting." I pick my battles carefully now. Compared to how I was ten years ago, my fuse is a mile long.

In my early twenties, I had a very painful experience. I decided I didn't want to live in pain anymore, so I began a pursuit of spirituality for the next twenty years, and I developed inside myself a very strong place of contentment. Since then, I've realized that there's nothing that can pull me from this place of contentment unless I allow it to, and I will not allow it. When you're with someone and they get angry, and that person makes you angry, it escalates the conversation. If a person gets angry and you *don't* get angry, it minimizes the conversation, and you get back to more of the facts.

Just the other day we were going somewhere, and I was wearing something my wife didn't like, and she got really emotional. We got into the car, and the car was quiet for maybe ten or fifteen minutes. Then she took her hand and put it on my hand, and I knew it was finished. I refused to be a part of her anger, so it got minimized very quickly.

Marriage is a marathon. Is what you're fighting about today still going to be important at the end of the race?

After ten years of marriage, I still haven't perfected the skill of not sweating the small stuff, but I really try. I say that if it's not harmful or illegal, then let it go.

❖

It helps to project a little bit into the future and think, *Do I want to make this permanent? Because if I say this, it's going to hurt. Is that really what I want?*

❖

They say the devil's in the details, and I think the devil really is in the details in marriage. Bad things happen when you lose sight of the big picture.

We went through a terrible time when I was pregnant. One of us wanted to keep the baby, and the other didn't. We had to accept, in a bad situation, that both of us were right. In a good, healthy relationship you can accept that the other one is right, and so are you, and it doesn't have to be one way or the other. I don't have to give ground in a very important situation, and neither does he. You have to make peace with the way it is and have patience to see how it all shakes out in twenty years. This is how you learn to grow up in a marriage.

Don't be so worried about protecting what you think is your turf or about the right way to do things. Take a step back, take a deep breath, and ask yourself whether, in the big scheme of things, it really matters. Is it worth having conflict over? Or is it worth keeping the peace? You don't want to do that at the expense of being a doormat, but at the same time, you have to recognize the fact that you're going to have conflicts over stupid stuff, and is it really worth it?

I think you can tell the difference between a temporary fight and something that's more serious. When my wife and I went through a bad patch, I was always looking beyond that. It's intangible, but even when it was difficult, I really loved her, I was stimulated by her, and I couldn't imagine being with anybody else. If I look at the relationships I know that have fallen apart, in most of the cases, the people came to a point where they couldn't be in the same room because there was all this experience and this well of emotion they couldn't control. In our case, I never had that. It never got to that point, even during those bad times. I felt like what we were going through did not define our relationship.

We're approaching fifty now, and we're dealing with friends and family who have cancers and those kinds of things. I try to think about if I were in that situation. If I had a year or six months to live, or my wife did, would that really be important to me? Often times I have to answer, "Well no, it wouldn't." So, why am I living my life as if it's important now? Sometimes forcing yourself into those exercises, saying those mantras to yourself, can actually change the way you feel about something.

Apologies and forgiveness are worth learning.

Apologies might not play a role every time, but the willingness to apologize if you're wrong must be an expectation. You have to have a history, if you were out of line, to be willing to apologize. And it has to be a genuine apology, not, "I'm sorry you made me so mad."

My husband and I had to work on apologies. I'd tell him I was sorry about something, but he'd keep harping on the subject. Then I'd say, "Okay, tell me which apology is going to be meaningful to you. Do you want me to say it ten times or a hundred times? Tell me which apology you're going to accept, and I'll get there, but I meant the first one when I said it." Sometimes when you're angry it can be hard to hear the apology, but it's important to learn how.

After a fight, my husband wants to say he's sorry right away and move on. That's stereotypically male, I think, wanting to have peace, but I'm not interested in that apology if he's not going to change his behavior. The apology doesn't mean anything if the same thing is going to happen again.

I'm not sure I'd believe it if someone told this to me, but my husband and I don't have the need for many apologies in our relationship. Someone may lose their temper, and that's not cool. In that case, the apology comes sincerely and is accepted readily, and then it's really let go.

When we have emotional outbursts, they don't go for days and weeks. It's like, *Okay, we had this thing, tempers flared, now let's move on.* The next day I say, "Give me a kiss, I gotta go to work." It wasn't like that in the beginning, but we don't hold on to grudges and bad feelings anymore.

One of the things I've always appreciated about my wife is that whenever we argue, it comes and goes. It's like a thunderstorm. The next morning it is gone. On rare occasions it will be brought up again, but for the most part, neither one of us dwells on it or comes back and brings up the same thing. It's always stuff for the moment.

I think having a bad memory is quite a good asset in a marriage. If you remember every tiny little thing that ever went wrong or every argument, then it would be a nightmare and you'd never go forward. As long as it's nothing big like someone having an affair, then having a bad memory is sometimes useful.

Forgiveness is key for my wife and me. I think the ability to forgive is the most significant trait you need in a successful marriage. There might be stewing for a little while, but the forgiveness is there, and I think it has to be a decision. Either I'm going to stay angry about this, or I'm going to let it go. You have to make a choice.

Couples who know each other really well may fight less than couples who don't.

Even after twenty-six years, one of the things that keeps our marriage very strong is that my wife and I talk, talk, talk all the time. It creates more understanding. We get to know each other really well. Then if there's something I do or say that she doesn't like or doesn't agree with, she might better understand the reason I would do it or say it.

My husband has a stronger personality than I do, and that was part of the reason I fell in love with him. But when we got into the relationship, ironically that became a source of conflict. Over the course of our relationship I've learned who he is, and I've accepted it.

My wife and I don't argue much anymore. When we talk about our arguing style, it sounds like there are a lot more than there were. In the last twelve years together, I bet we've only had three good arguments that lasted for more than thirty minutes.

I'm very expressive, and my husband is the opposite. He likes to think things through, and the more I push, the more reticent he'll be. In the early days, I'd know there was something wrong, and we'd end up screaming at each other to break the logjam, and it was exhausting and hurtful. After a while, I learned to express myself, then wait and let him eventually open up. It took patience on my part and recognizing who he is, not bending to get him to be who I want him to be. These days we almost never fight.

After you're married for a while, you find on certain issues it's not worth pressing anymore. Forcing a decision becomes more damaging than what it's all about. These days, if my wife feels something is going to be too hard on me, she backs off. And I do the same for her.

I've heard it said that if people don't fight it means there's a time bomb, something ticking underneath. It's not true for my husband and me at all. We disagree all the time, but we don't have arguments.

Sometimes my husband and I will be deep into a fight, and one of us will make a face or say something ridiculous, and we just start laughing—and it changes. Actually, nothing's changed, but it lightens the load. For the most part, our fights are stupid miscommunications that escalate. We don't ever really want to be fighting, so any course to get us out of it will help.

I used to pay a lot of attention to when my wife was up or down. I'd constantly ask, "What's wrong, what's wrong?" Now I don't worry about it. I've learned that if I ask her what's wrong and she says, "Nothing," then I believe her and move on.

We've been together for eight years, and my wife and I might have had two arguments. Conflict for us is very, very rare. That's part of our chemistry. We respect and allow the independence of the other person. There are a lot of things she does that I would never do, but I have no interest in trying to intervene in her habits, methods, language, friends, whatever it might be. She respects me in the same way. We disagree about a lot, but we don't infringe.

You're supposed to be partners. You're supposed to be there to help each other through life. There will always be conflict, but that's just part of finding common goals. If you approach life as partners, you'll find a way to work through it.

Chapter 3

....

ROOMMATE ISSUES

Matrimony is a process by which
the grocer acquired an account the florist had.
—Francis Rodman

I DON'T HAVE KIDS, but I'm aware of a parenting technique called modeling, where you teach your kids how to behave by showing them what good behavior looks like. From what I can tell, it means that if you don't want your kids to swear, for example, then you shouldn't swear around them.

If you don't want them to eat like barnyard animals, then you should use good table manners in front of them.

If you want them to share their toys, then they should see you sharing your speedboat.

This seems like some nonsense, if you ask me. If acting the right way is acting the right way, then do it all the time! And don't waste it on your kids. They're looking at their phones anyway, not at you.

Some people feel free to be their worst selves at home. Why bother shaving, bathing, washing the windows, doing laundry, taking out the trash, unclogging the sink, cleaning the grill, scrubbing the grout, or doing anything else when you are at home in your sanctuary, free from the prying eyes of civilized society?

These are "roommate issues," and they are another element of marriage to be navigated. Living together means you're sharing space and possessions with another person. One partner's behavior affects the other.

Do happy couples argue about housekeeping and chores? Why should these things be important enough to start a fight?

The couples interviewed advise that manners play a role. It turns out that "please" and "thank you" are powerful words. They also said that even trivial things sometimes require negotiation, and it can be worthwhile to think about changing the way you do some things as you learn to live together.

After all, roommate issues relate directly to creating a life at home where both parties can live in peace and comfort. And that's not really trivial at all.

We're all just a bunch of animals, especially when no one's looking. Living with another person can be challenging.

Housekeeping is probably our biggest problem on the small scale. My wife and I have a very different sense of what's neat and orderly.

The way my wife handles the recycling bin in our house drives me nuts. There's one recycling bin under the kitchen sink, and she just throws stuff in there. She doesn't knock down the boxes. She loads up that bin with as much as it can take, and when it's full, she just keeps going. It fills up quickly, and she never empties it, so then I empty it, and stuff is flying everywhere because it's literally stacked twice as high as the actual bin. I actually empty it when she's not around, because if she were around, I'd say something I would regret. I've mentioned it to her, but she keeps on doing it.

My husband is incredibly anal about organization. He complains about me all the time. My friends, however, think he's crazy, because we have two children and have the most clutter-free, immaculate house ever. It doesn't even look like children live here except in their rooms. He'd really like everything to have its perfect place, and I think that's nearly impossible.

I cover every surface with stuff. There's never a surface that doesn't have something sitting on it. My husband will go through and move the magazines off the table so he doesn't have to look at everything laying around, but within seconds, without even thinking about it, I'll set something down on it.

My wife does chores on a schedule that is much more active than it needs to be. I think the house is *too* taken care of. The laundry and dishes are running all the time. The trash gets taken out way too early—we could definitely fit more in. She doesn't stop working until about 8:30 at night, and up until that point she's just constantly doing chores. I'm appreciative that she does these things, but on the other hand, sometimes I wish she'd wait a little longer. Everything doesn't need to be done in such a hurry. On nights when I need some quiet time, I hide things from her like the laundry baskets so that she'll relax—and then I can relax, too.

My husband is deep-down tidier than I am. I think sometimes he must walk in and think, *Oh, it's messy in here. It's chaotic.* I know he thinks it, but he doesn't say anything, which I appreciate.

My husband leaves his empty beer bottles for recycling at the top of the stairs to the basement, and it drives me insane. We keep the beer cases in the basement out of sight. He'll put his empties at the top of the stairs or leave them on the counter instead of taking them straight down to the basement, and they don't move. There are always bottles hanging around. He'll hide them, or tuck them behind stuff, but I know they're there.

❖

My husband always has all this stuff in his pockets, so I got him a nice box by the door for his stuff—keys, coins, cufflinks, old receipts. It's a neutral color to match the décor, and against my better judgment, I put it in one of the alcoves for display things. But he's filled it up now. It's overflowing, and there's a little sea of items around it. I tease him about the fact that it's "his" area, but it really needs to be sorted out.

Living together will immediately require give and take. You're going to have two people living in the same space, with different habits and different opinions. You're going to have conflict over whose stuff goes where, if you have separate toothpastes or one, or if you have your own corner of the house and how you're keeping it. That's not going to change just because you're married.

I remember during premarital counseling with our pastor, he talked about how the dishwasher is often a source of conflict for couples. My husband and I are expecting a baby now and saving for ridiculously expensive daycare, so we're taking our lunch to work every day. As a result, there are about a thousand pieces of Tupperware when we run the dishwasher.

My husband says he doesn't have a half hour to spend organizing the dishwasher, so he just shoves stuff in there. Then I end up getting annoyed and reorganizing the whole thing. It's funny, but our pastor was dead-on.

When I met my wife, I was intimidated by how neat she was then, and she still is. Generally, our whole house is very clean, but she lets me keep my office just the way I want to, which I really appreciate. My desk and my office are a mess, and she rarely makes a comment.

My wife is organizationally challenged. She knows where everything is, but her idea of organizing is to put all of a certain general type of thing in a drawer. So, the "household items" drawer will have, for example, appliance manuals, light bulbs, tools, and screws. I used to reorganize and think I was doing her a huge favor, but then she'd be useless when I was like, "Where are the pliers?" She'd say, "I don't know. I used to keep them all in this one drawer, and now I can't find them." Now I just reorganize the fridge every once in a while as a small form of protest.

I'm almost to the point of insanity about cleanliness, but I've had to let go of that over the years because it's just not rational. It's not good for me, and it drives my husband nuts. There are only so many things you can sterilize.

My husband wouldn't believe this, but I really cater to his needs about how everything in our house is put away and clutter-free. I was never messy, but I'm a packrat. Since we got married, I really make a conscious effort to work toward being more like him, because if it's not orderly or clutter-free, he won't be comfortable. I try, but I don't think it's up to his standards yet. Maybe another ten years of marriage will do it.

The ideal combination would be to have one spouse who cares about everything in the house to the tiniest degree and another person who doesn't care about anything. That would be smooth sailing.

A quick word about bathroom etiquette.

Whoever's in the bathroom, the door still goes closed. I don't care how many years you've been married, that door goes closed.

All my life, and throughout my first marriage, I would lift the toilet seat, go to the bathroom, and walk away. I used to think that what my wife wanted me to do was close the lid, but really it was about the seat. For the benefit of other men, this is because you fall through if you sit down when the seat is up. I learned this the hard way: I did it myself in the dark one night. I didn't really understand that until my second marriage, believe it or not.

As far as bodily functions go, over the years I think we've let that slip a little bit. By the time you have all these kids and dogs who poop and pee, the bodily functions are everywhere. Our children find it all very funny. We're up to our elbows in that kind of reality, but we still try to exercise a lot of self-control.

My wife doesn't like me walking in while she's using the bathroom. For some reason, it doesn't bother me as much. I don't have a hang-up about it, but, man, she really doesn't like it.

❖

My husband still closes the bathroom door after nine years. He's polite to me, and it makes me feel respected. In some contexts, we treat each other with the same courtesy you'd give a stranger, which a lot of people don't do.

You and your spouse didn't have the same mother (at least I hope you didn't). You're going to do some things differently.

My husband is really particular about things. He likes things a certain way, and he won't let go. For example, I do the laundry, and he'll come in and ask why I'm putting something in cold water. Or I don't fold his socks the way he likes, or I don't button his shirts right. He's got a lot of little things like that, and I'm like, "Why am I explaining this to you? I'm doing the laundry. You don't need to be in here. Go away."

My wife went back to work full-time recently, so now once a week I make dinner for the family. Some things I feel like I can do okay, but I've learned I can't do things my way because the family won't eat it. I do appreciate the quality of my wife's meals. I can tell it's a better meal to have fresh vegetables, for example, and I appreciate it. But there's stuff she cares about that I don't. I don't care if some of the vegetables are cut bigger and some are smaller, or if there are stems in the spinach. I'm mindful of what she doesn't like to see, but even after twenty years, we haven't totally worked it out.

I sometimes say that I have two kids at home: my daughter and my husband. When we need to go somewhere, it's like getting two kids out of the house, because I have my big kid and my little kid. He lives for the moment, and I live by a calendar. I'm like, "We need to be at work now. We cannot dilly-dally. Put her hat on, put her gloves on, stop playing games. It's not tickle time."

Years ago, when our kids were younger, I went to a conference where there were a lot of families. It was a revelation, because I saw that the "new modern man" was a tyrant. My husband, on the other hand, never criticized the way I changed a diaper or worked with our kids. It was my territory. He gave me the kind of respect that men give men. He wouldn't go to his boss and tell him how to run the company, but some men do that with their wives. My husband respected me and left me alone to make decisions. I literally ran into the house after that conference and said to him, "Thank you for leaving me alone!"

If I'm heating something up in the microwave, I'll throw my food on a paper towel instead of getting out a dish, and that drives my wife nuts. Men aren't as process-oriented as women, so they take shortcuts. The woman might be like "Hey, there's a process here." She'll tell me, for example, that there are five steps involved in getting to a certain point. But I'm thinking, *I'll get there in two and a half.* We're all trying to get to the same point, but I might take a more relaxed way of getting there.

I think women are natural organizers and prioritizers, and men are less so. We can clearly see in our mind's eye how something needs to be done, like it's on an Excel spreadsheet that sorts it out. We want to have our husbands follow our lead, but men don't seem to want to do that. They feel like they're browbeaten or whipped if they take direction from their wives. This is true for my husband and me, at least, and I see it with my friends, too.

The straw that breaks the camel's back on a daily basis for my husband and me is dinner. We both work full-time, and he doesn't cook. It's always a stress on me to cook dinner when I get home. I'd die to come home and have dinner made, but a healthy dinner, not junk food or frozen food. He has taken on more responsibility for it by learning some basics. I want it my way, though. I'd like to have him in the driver's seat, but I want to be included in the decision, so it's a tough one to delegate.

My husband and I are each fussy about different things. He's very good at *starting* to do laundry, but he never finishes, and it drives me crazy. He'll have piles of laundry around the house that are half-folded or ironed, and that doesn't bother him. Meanwhile, if I come into the house and don't hang up my coat, it bugs him. Does that make sense? Over time I've decided I'd rather not fight about it, but it still annoys me.

When we first got married, there were things that set off little alarm bells for me, like which way the toilet paper would hang. I didn't care which way it went, but it was obviously a big deal to my wife. You see those little glimpses of things when you're first married, and the reasonably perceptive person will wonder what that could lead to, but I decided not to make an issue of that thing in particular.

We've been married for almost twenty-five years now, and just the other day, I hung the toilet paper backward to see what would happen. Sure enough, the next time I came in, it was flipped around.

Yes, you have to say it.
Communicating about work around the house is necessary, if not always pleasant.

My husband and I used to fight about chores, but not as much now because I've resigned myself to the way he is. It's not that he's lazy.

He's a man. He doesn't see that the dishwasher needs to be emptied. I don't look at it as a favor he's doing for me. It's our house, so we both have a stake in it and its cleanliness and organization. It bothers me if I have to ask him to help out, because it's like, he lives here, too.

He is getting better, though. If the laundry is on the bed and needs to be folded, he'll fold it. Or if we run out of dog food, he'll go get it. We've made some progress.

I'm a clean person, but not as clean as my wife. She runs a tighter ship than I do, and that's where the arguments come from. I'll tell her that I understand she wants me to do more, but she's going to have to tell me if she wants it done ahead of the schedule I have in my head. She doesn't want to have to tell me, though. She wants me to notice.

Today I stood up all day. I was cleaning out one room, doing laundry, moving some things around, and all day long I was busy doing stuff. Four or five times I looked over at my husband, and he was sitting in a chair reading a magazine. Some of that's fine if he's not working, but taking care of the house and family should be a partnership. When I have to ask him for help, that still bothers me.

I used to have a friend, and her marriage was an unhappy one. She used to tell me all the terrible things her husband would do. When they were fighting, he'd say "Well, what do you want?" And then she would respond, "Well, if I have to tell you, then that's the whole problem." My friend thought her husband should just know and read her mind. That's asking for trouble if you think someone's going to be able to read your mind. You *do* have to talk about what you want, and you have to make it very clear.

I don't want to be delegating and giving out chores to my husband. I certainly don't want to be a nag. But women multitask, and men don't. You can't be afraid to ask for help. Instead of getting resentful because he's not helping, I've realized I just have to ask him. Then, when I do ask him for help, he doesn't give me attitude. He's happy to do it. I wonder why I have to ask, but I honestly don't think it occurs to him.

Even in a good marriage, one kind of person will see that the dishes need to be done or the furniture needs a quick dusting. So, I'll say to my husband, "Can you do the dusting while I'm gone today?" And he might say "What do you mean, it needs dusting?" He's not being negligent. He just doesn't see it, and we can't read each other's minds.

My wife and I split up the chores at home, but I could do more, I'm sure. I know I could. She does all the laundry, for example, because I screw it up. I do stuff by nature that I want to do, that sometimes can be more fun to do, and that may not be the priority that she has. Like I may work on something outside, when what she really wants is something fixed inside. The other day I cleaned half the house, and she did half the house. She does the laundry, I make the bed, she does the cooking, I clean up. I do what I'm told to do. Some things aren't worth fighting over.

An agreeable division of labor can help keep the peace.

I have never pushed a lawnmower in my life, and I don't intend to. I do the chores inside, and my husband does them outside, and that works for us.

In my husband's family, his mom waited on his dad hand and foot, so that's what he expects. That's how my parents are, too. My mom waits on my dad, she gets up from the table and brings him more food and more drinks. He drops his dirty clothes on the floor, and she picks them up. I'm not going to do that. I don't think that's part of the deal, and I'm still trying to orient my husband to that fact.

One of the reasons I'm in a marriage is to make my husband happy, but sometimes I get resentful when I feel like he's not working as hard as I am.

In our house, we split the chores; I do the interior stuff and my husband deals with the exterior. In the beginning it was tough, and we used to fight about it a lot. I like my house to be clean, and it takes about three hours to clean it. By the second hour of cleaning I used to get angry, because he'd be done with his stuff and watching football while I was still working.

Sometimes it doesn't feel equal because I do the chores of keeping the house clean, emptying the dishwasher, making sure the house stays the way it is, and I'll have to remind my husband to do his part. It doesn't always feel fair, but if I wrote it all down, it would probably be pretty equal.

My husband and I don't have tension in our marriage in the division of household labor. Maybe if I got a full-time job outside the home, that might change. But because I can do the housework, I don't mind. And we have clearly set boundaries, in that he does cars, computers, and everything outside. It's not a vague, "Oh, do you need help doing something?" He does stuff that I don't do, and for us it works to have those categories. There's no question about who's going to take care of what.

I take care of most of the housekeeping, but my husband does all the beautification like gardening and decorating in our home. I didn't grow up in a home where we decorated. That wasn't in our budget. We worried about lunch and a pair of shoes, so now I'd rather spend my money on clothes and shoes and purses. He wanted to decorate, so he did the painting, the coloring, the accent pillows, the headboard. I didn't pick out any of it, but I appreciate it.

I always wanted to marry my best friend and someone who was an equal life partner. My husband and I have someone who mows the lawn and someone who cleans our house, so we don't have too many chores to split up. The chores that we do have, we split equally. We each cook one thing for the week, and we eat those two things all week long. Our friends are a lot more gendered than we are, but I never envisioned marriage that way. I'm glad my husband agrees.

**Just like they taught us in kindergarten,
courtesy and kindness
make life together more pleasant.**

I expect my husband to treat me the same way he'd treat the Queen of England, except I don't demand that he calls me Your Majesty.

Manners are important to my wife and me at home because we have kids watching, for one thing. But that's not the only reason. What are you going to do when the kids leave home? Walk around in your underwear scratching yourself?

Manners are very important. You don't burp, you don't pick your nose, you don't do anything at home that you wouldn't do outside in that regard. Who you are in your family is who you are. That's no way to act if you behave better outside than you do at home.

Manners don't have to be overdone, and it's not a formal thing. It gets to be natural, if you do it long enough. It gets to be a habit. You have to realize that your partner's not an appendage of you. They're another person, and you need to treat them with respect.

Every once in a while, I think about myself as I'm eating dinner and wonder about how I look in my shorts and tee shirt. I never look like the dad on that old show *Father Knows Best*, for example. I mean, I'm always clothed. In our house, it's no shirt, no shoes, no service But I sometimes wonder if it would show more respect for my wife and my family to look a little better at the dinner table.

A few years ago, my wife bought me a pair of elastic-waist lounge pants. I'm like, "No way. I am not wearing those, ever. Take them straight back." Believe me, I work at home, and I'm not that concerned about how I look when I'm sitting in the office. But I just don't want to go down that road. I wear jeans and a turtleneck every day. And I shave once a week. I do have standards. Don't let anyone tell you otherwise.

Manners are important, but I think I'm slipping a little. I think I'm becoming a little more like my mother, a little bitchier and more short-tempered with my husband than I would like to be. We're polite, and we say "please" and "thank you" and "I love you" five times a day easily, always. But I'd like not to be so short-tempered with him. I'm working on that.

If you don't show respect for each other, you'll lose ground. This may sound like a Richard Scarry children's book, but we say "please" and "thank you." We do it for each other, but we're also role models for our children—although we were married for seven years before we had kids, and I can't say there were big changes in that area after we had them.

It's not an outmoded convention to say "please" and "thank you." It sends a message twenty-four hours a day that how I act toward my wife is important, and how she perceives me is important. For me to say "please," or to say the food tastes good, is going to send a completely different message than if I say nothing and just hold out my plate for more.

❖

Manners for manners' sake are not important. What is important is that I'm going to go that extra mile, even when I don't feel like it, to treat my wife well, to treat her in a way that acknowledges she's doing something for me or that she's done something important. It means respect. It means some amount of regard for the other person, what they've done, what they've been through.

Courtesy is very important. It just makes sense that if you respect your spouse, you treat them with courtesy, and you deserve to be treated that way in return.

My family makes an effort to eat dinner together at night. I know there are people who think, *We're so busy, we couldn't possibly eat together every night.* It's okay for them to grab something out of the fridge, say nothing, leave dirty dishes, and come back later. But when I come home, I know my wife has dinner planned. Even if I don't feel like it, even if I've had a bad day, even if the kids are not getting along, she's gone to the effort of making dinner. So, we're going to sit down, have dinner, and see how it mixes up. Even if it's not stellar family time, we'll see how it works out. By that, there's an acknowledgment that her effort was worthwhile.

Every once in a while, I don't feel like it, or it takes a little extra effort to be courteous. We all have bad moments where we fall down. But it's the one day out of six months where things are really bad, and you make the extra effort to carry that out, where it makes the difference.

Chapter 4

....

MONEY

Marriage halves our griefs, doubles our joys,
and quadruples our expenses.
—English Proverb

M ONEY IS ONE OF THE TOP ISSUES couples fight about. To be clear,
they're usually not fighting because there's *too much* money in
the relationship. It's pretty much always that there's not enough. Even
the millionaire set can find themselves with the realization that they
just don't have quite as much as they need.

So, would winning the lottery help? Surely getting a windfall in
the hundreds of millions would fix it. Well, according to statistics, lottery winners do divorce less than nonwinners do…but only by about 3
percent, which isn't too impressive.

If money can't solve money problems, then what's going on?

Money is tied to our priorities in life, and those priorities come into sharp focus when we have financial disagreements. To complicate
things even more, money discussions often get emotional, as they can

be influenced by childhood experiences or the way one's parents handled money.

For example, if your parents were big spenders who lived on credit cards and a second mortgage to support a luxurious lifestyle, then you may have some spending habits you inherited without realizing it. On the other hand, if your parents were environmentalists who shopped only at thrift stores and believed it was wrong to buy new goods that only ended up in landfills, then you may have inherited spending habits that lean in the other direction.

How can spouses come together when they have competing financial priorities? According to our happy couples, solving money matters requires discussion about the values and goals you have individually and for your family. For some, building reliable budgets and systems for their personal finances has removed a lot of stress.

Once those systems are in place and spouses learn to trust each other, many of the couples say that money can become a nonissue, no longer a source of conflict at all.

Managing money for two is more complicated than managing money for one.

Money is the biggest hidden anxiety in our relationship.

We were so broke when we got married. I remember going to the grocery store and thinking, *Oh my gosh, this casserole has three different spices in it that I don't have. That's going to run up the bill.* I remember being shocked at the cost of running a household. It was expensive.

When we were younger, sometimes there just wasn't enough money at the end of the month. I was always very self-conscious because I didn't want my husband to think that his income wasn't good enough. His income was always very good, but we had so much going out the door with the kids. It was always the kids.

If you brought two strangers together and told them to come up with a business plan and a financial strategy, I predict it wouldn't be a big deal. They'd figure it all out in an hour or two. For some reason, though, husbands and wives can get really tense about managing money together.

I get in trouble sometimes for not showing enough concern about our finances. It's not that I don't care, but I think my wife's terror alert goes to red before mine.

I remember when we first got married and I stopped working, I felt so strange about spending my husband's money. We decided I wouldn't work when we started to have children, but before then I'd been making my own decisions and budgeting my own money and buying my own clothes. When he was the only one bringing home a paycheck, it felt so odd.

My husband isn't American, so when I convinced him to stay in the country when we were dating, he wasn't legally allowed to work. His family was no longer paying any of his expenses, and he literally had no money. He was too proud to ask for any, and he felt shame for not having it. I tried to make sure he had everything he needed and would give him cash from time to time. When he started to work and make money, I realized what a power differential that had been and how bad it made him feel.

There have been times when my wife has been concerned about how much money we have coming in, and I want to avoid the conversation because I feel like I should be making more than I do. It makes me feel a little smaller than I want to feel. I don't feel like I'm being a good husband who's supposed to be the provider, I guess.

When we didn't have much money, it was an area of conflict because my husband and I wanted to spend money on completely different things. Spending money on the house was a low priority for him, and it was a huge one for me. He thought it was fine that the walls were lime green and we had a tiny, horrible kitchen. We couldn't afford to redo the whole kitchen, but it would have been nice to freshen it up or paint the cupboards. We just couldn't agree.

Agreement won't happen automatically. You'll have to make an effort to communicate about money and priorities.

Real life is real life, whether you're married or not. Just because you found the love of your life doesn't mean that all the other drudgeries aren't going to hit home, like having to pay bills, having difficulties with friends, or feeling the pressures of school or a career. All that stuff is going to be there. I think a lot of people go into marriage thinking they're going to have a whole new life. They'll pool their incomes and it'll all be different. As silly as that sounds, I know some people who believed that marriage would fix all that.

Dealing with money together held some surprises for my wife and me. We didn't have a whole lot of it starting out. In one way we had more than before, because we had two salaries. But having collective priorities was an adjustment. You have to think about two people, not one, for your daily needs—for retirement, for buying a house, and for making any major purchase. The decisions you make affect you in both the short term and the long term. For me, it was having to adjust to a whole new perspective.

For my wife and me, there were some misunderstandings and bumpy terrain in dealing with money in the early days. I get the sense that's normal in figuring out what's reasonable and responsible to spend on yourself, each other, and the family.

My wife and I are very different in terms of how we handle money. I am a miser. I like to hold money, and I'm also obsessed with global climate change and not wasting energy. My wife thinks money should be spent and energy should be used. I complain about it periodically, with little effect.

My husband flies all the time for his job, and he isn't good about claiming his frequent flier miles, which we could be using for ourselves. He also isn't good about turning in receipts for expenses he incurs while on business travel. We should be getting reimbursed, and it really annoys me that he won't do a little extra paperwork to get that cash back. It's money down the drain. I think, *I could have bought a pair of shoes with that.*

My husband and I got together when we were very young, and we've always shared everything. When I stopped working to be home with our children, even though he was earning the money, I considered that my money, too. What's funny is that sometimes these days if I take a little part-time job and get a tiny bit of money, I'll squirrel it away and say, "That's mine." I guess that that means my husband is more generous than I am.

The world has sped up so much faster than it did watching our parents with finances. I remember every Saturday we'd go to the ATM so my dad could take out the cash that he needed for the week.

Now it's all on the cards, you don't need the cash, you can buy what you need immediately, so I look at our bank accounts daily. My wife and I are serious about managing our money together. We respect each other enough to let the other one know what we're doing. We talk about our wants versus our needs, what the priorities are, and what the time frame is that we need things by. We have a daily game plan on expenditures.

Before my wife and I got married, our pastor counseled us to us to have a weekly meeting with each other to discuss three things: our checkbook, our calendar, and our relationship. In other words, how are we doing with our money, how are we doing with our time, and how are things with us? Time and money are precious commodities. The way we use and spend them says a whole lot about what we value. As a married couple, those values are something you want to talk about frequently.

If you want to start a fight, one surefire technique is to spend a lot of money without consulting your spouse.

A few years ago we were in the market for a new car. Instead of sitting down with figuring out what we could afford, my husband went to a car show by himself and bought a truck, out of the blue. I stewed for a long time about that one.

Our most recent fight was about money. My husband spent quite a bit on stereo equipment without telling me. It was the lack of communication that bothered me. I handle our finances, and he didn't consult me or even ask my opinion.

How could he spend that much on something without telling me? It struck me as kind of dishonest. Then I thought that if he spent that much on himself, then I deserved something, too, but I didn't buy myself anything. Communication could have prevented that argument.

If you have differing ideas about what to spend a limited amount of your money on, never make a decision on your own. There's got to be a decent compromise—like we won't get a new car, but we can get a used car. Or we can replace four of our leaky windows instead of eight. Making a big financial decision on your own can be a really dangerous move.

Watching my parents really helped me figure out how I was going to handle finances with my wife. I vividly remember driving back with my dad after he picked up our family's first VCR. We walked in the door to a tornado, with my mother saying, "What did you buy? How could you possibly buy that? You don't care about our finances and our future!" My parents had no problem fighting right in front of us. It happened again when my dad bought a microwave without talking to her. He just figured he was the man of the house, and it was his money.

Now don't get me wrong, my mom used that microwave every single day. She saw the value in it, and it helped them get through that fight and future fights. But when he spent the money without any consultation beforehand, the fights were just incredible. That VCR darn near landed them in divorce court. Those experiences helped drive a lot of the respect I have for my wife now. I don't want those fights. It's very easy to avoid that.

Go on, blame your parents.
We learn some of our most basic attitudes about money during childhood.

When it comes to money, I didn't realize how much my husband and I were both products of our environment. I have my dad's attitude toward money—the good and the bad—and my husband's attitudes were a lot like his father's. We never thought about that coming into the marriage. In time I came to see that was true, and it explained some of the disagreements we had.

I joke with my husband that he's turned me into a spender. His father died when he was young, and his mother felt like you should live while you can and spend it while you've got it. There's no point in saving if you could be run over by a bus tomorrow, and that's where he gets this attitude.

We do have some savings and retirement accounts, but I would like to save more money than we do. He's turned me into a spender now on our vacations in particular. When we're on vacation, we're going to enjoy ourselves, even if we have a bit of an over-run on the credit card. Generally we agree that fun comes first. If we need a new sofa and we have to choose between that and a holiday, then we agree now that the sofa can wait until next year.

Money is never much of an issue for my husband and me. We both come from homes where there was never a lot, and we know we should never spend beyond our means. We've fallen into a pretty good pattern where he brings home the money, I bank it, and if we know something is coming up, we save for that.

Both my wife's parents and mine were raised during the Depression. You don't just throw things away. I know men who talk about their wives spending money shopping, but my wife doesn't do that, so we don't have conflict about it.

Money always presented a lot of pressure for me. My mom equates financial success with being a good person. My family is Southern, Republican, and Baptist, and it's assumed you'll drive a nice car and go to church. If you're a good person, you're financially successful, and vice versa.

My wife, our marriage, and our kids have helped refocus me, though. I got into job trouble at one point that was stressful, but I had to ask myself if I was going to wake up tomorrow and have work and an income that pays the mortgage and feeds us. Well, yeah. It wasn't that bad. Was I going to have an income that would put a Range Rover in the driveway by Christmas? No, but I realized I can't be worried about success, other than knowing we have food on the table and everybody's okay. It's been very helpful to have that refocusing. Even though the pressure I grew up with is still there, I don't feel so consumed by it.

My wife's family didn't have much growing up, so she appreciates everything we've ever gotten. After we were married for two years, we moved out of our apartment and bought a townhouse. She was amazingly appreciative to have her first set of stairs. She's a very open and loving person when it comes to finances. She has no expectations of me in that regard, and it's made life easier. We don't argue a lot about money.

Yours, mine, or ours?
How you bank doesn't seem to matter,
as long as you're open with each other
about financial matters in general.

You have to approach managing money together like a business where you're legal partners. A Chief Financial Officer should be assigned.

The other corporate officer should receive regular reports. There should be a budget and guidelines on spending.

My wife and I have different attitudes about money: I save, she spends. In the old days, I used to give her money. Then she started making her own money, so I stopped giving it to her, and she set up a separate bank account. She had her money, and she spent it the way she wanted to. That actually worked. Now she's not making as much money, so we're having to readjust again.

Early in our marriage, my wife made it sound like pooling your money was an old way of doing things, like an old attitude that wasn't progressive. I think her idea was that each person should be able to stand by themselves and carry half the load.

But I said, "Let's just throw it all in there." I know sometimes it can go awry, but sharing everything works for us.

The first few years, we kept our accounts completely separate from each other, but we fought about money more then. Now we pool everything, and I manage it. It's an open book between us, and we really don't fight about money anymore.

I don't think it's important to pool your money. Even though my wife and I have joint accounts, I can picture how it would work to keep it separate. At the same time, I've known several people who had separate accounts, and it ended in disaster. One person was always broke and borrowing from the other one, for example. Or the reasons that would lead you to maintain separate accounts in the first place may mean that you have something to hide, or you've got some spending habit you don't want to share. I'd look at that.

I wouldn't stand in the way of anyone who wanted a prenuptial agreement, or separate bank accounts, or a legal arrangement to keep assets separate. But I will say that by doing that, you may be establishing a certain level of mistrust right from the beginning. That separateness could keep you from finding compromise or working together to solve a financial situation.

I know the reason my husband and I don't fight about money is that we value it the same way. Neither of us needs it to be happy, but we enjoy it and the material things we can buy. We both work really hard for it, too, so there's a respect for it.

Not everybody is good with a spreadsheet. Sometimes it works best for one partner to manage the money.

Last night I told my wife I needed a new suit. I only have one, and I need another one. She knew that it was going to cost about $1,500, and she said, "Well, we can't do that now. It's going to have to wait a few months." I didn't say anything, but I was thinking, "That bugs me." I turned into a ten-year-old. I know I just don't have all the information about why she said that. She's on top of it, and she knows more about our money than I do. Ultimately, I know she'll find a way to make it happen. She always finds a way.

I don't look at the money. My wife handles everything, and she's got it under control. I have no stress because I don't even open any bills, and my world is beautiful. She controls everything but doesn't make me feel like I'm being controlled. I think that's the mark of a great leader.

In terms of the big picture, we have an equal understanding. I handle the money, and my husband has a sense of our retirement account, for example, but he wouldn't know how much is in our bank accounts or what I spend on the house or groceries every week. He trusts me to take care of it.

I keep close track of our finances because my husband and I both spend money like water. We have big bills, and neither of us is really fantastic with money. I keep us in line by tracking it. I know where our money is, and I know if we spend too much.

I handle our finances. My husband is welcome to check out our accounts and the spreadsheet I update every week, but he doesn't pay any attention. I can tell you right now that he doesn't know if he has a balance on his credit card. He doesn't know what bills come and go, and the system works for us.

I don't need to know about every single decision my wife makes with our money. I don't want her to run up a huge credit card bill or take money away from the mortgage, the kids, or the kids' education. But she's shown by history that she doesn't do that, so I trust her to make those decisions. If she wants to go out with a friend or buy clothes, I don't worry about it.

My wife runs the house and finances, and I go to work every day and come home. I think it's great. There's no way I'd ever have survived this long without her. Every once in a while, I'll look at a bill and say, "Is this right?" We used to live in Dallas, and we were talking to some friends a while back with a $500 electric bill. I said, "Our bill is nowhere near that," and then my wife told me we pay $600. I said, "Really?" We each have our job descriptions, and we have a lot of confidence in each other.

After almost twenty-five years together, my wife and I never fight about money—ever. Early on we did have conflicts as we were adjusting to each other's saving and spending habits. Once you work through that and establish a base of trust, you've defined who's going to manage the accounts, and you agree on where the money's going, then you're on cruise control.

Remember that money has meaning. The way you spend now could be sending signals to your partner about your future.

Money addresses the vulnerability we all feel. Every single one of us, whether we're twenty or eighty years old, is afraid of starving to death, of not having the basics. These feelings are connected to money, and that's why it becomes such a hot subject.

Retirement is where there's real difficulty in our relationship because I'm fifty-two and my wife's forty-two. If I've got only eight more years that I'm going to be working, I've got to crank more into retirement now. But my wife is in the now. She's over-the-top in the now, anyway, as a person. She wants to travel and doesn't want to think about retirement. She says, "Don't age me," and, "You're fifty-two, *I'm* not fifty-two." I see that issue becoming bigger in the next few years for us.

I'm trying to think of how many guy friends I have who really would say they're in a happy marriage, and I can probably count them on one hand. By far the majority of couples I'm thinking of are people who don't know each other very well. They're getting 28 percent loans to buy $30,000 motorcycles, their wives are spending them out of house and home on shoes and clothes, and they're complaining about that. That's going to doom most people to failure. You're both messing with each other's future. That's really what you're doing.

But on the other hand, if you've got somebody who has the same priorities you do, who approaches your marriage like a partnership, who you've learned to trust, then I don't think you're going to have fights about money.

Chapter 5

....

PUBLIC AND PRIVATE

A good marriage is that in which
each appoints the other guardian of his solitude.
—Rainer Maria Rilke

T HE HUMAN BODY is both a marvelous machine...and a house of horrors. All manner of things can go wrong, especially by a certain age. It's all just biology, but somehow our ailments can be embarrassing, too, especially as you gain proximity to the bathing suit area.

Imagine going to the doctor and having to wonder if your problems are going to provide hilarious conversation material for her and her friends over cocktails at the end of the day. I don't know who invented the confidentiality rule for doctors, but that was a good idea.

Now, if behavioral codes exist for doctors, lawyers, and other professionals, aren't you entitled to at least the same consideration in your most personal, emotional life?

What are the rules about confidentiality in a marriage? Do married people change their behavior when they're in public, or should they be able to do, and share, whatever they want?

Most of the people interviewed agree that there are things in a marriage that are entitled to confidentiality. Some of the happy couples even laid out a shared philosophy, which got clarified after someone said too much and crossed the line.

The good news is that once the rules are hashed out, they're pretty easy to follow, and that makes getting together with friends a lot more fun. In fact, friendships outside the marriage are important, both for individuals and for couples. Once spouses learn where the danger zones are, then the marriage is protected, and friendships can flourish.

Everybody has soft spots.
Learn where your partner's are.

I had to learn that my wife doesn't want me to say things about her in public. I might think that something I was saying was innocent or unimportant, or even that I was sticking up for her. We're admittedly not the life of the party. Those kinds of people are more inclined to tell stories or personal things, and that would get us in trouble. We talk in public about safe subjects we agree on.

Once, my husband confided something intimate and personal with a mutual friend, somebody we both know well. I told him afterward that I believe those kinds of things are meant just for us, and that if he needs to confide in someone it should be with a professional, or a friend who's not also my friend. And he said, "Oh. I get it. Sorry." After that, he never did it again.

Women like to talk with each other about their husbands. I guess it's beneficial to hear that other people might be having similar issues or problems. I might say, "Oh, my husband does that, too," and I don't always talk about him in perfectly glowing terms. I'll admit that we fight, or maybe that he's messy. But I don't give a lot of details. One of the reasons I don't is that I wouldn't want my husband giving specifics to his friends about the things we fight about.

I'm in a book group with some other women, and we get together once a month. At the end of the evening, the conversation usually turns away from books to talking about our marriages and sex.

Other women seem to like to talk about that, but I don't, because I wouldn't want my husband talking about that part of our life with other people.

I certainly tell my friends things about my marriage, but they're not things that my husband doesn't know about. I joke with my fiftysomething friends about the fact that my husband and I are not "in lust" as much, and we laugh about that because we're all hormonally challenged. I don't feel like that's a big marital secret.

For me, a lot has to do with who you're telling: my sister-in-law, for example. She's not discreet, and I don't want her telling all her friends something she might learn about my family, like that my daughter is struggling in school. My husband does know she's a gossip, but I'll still have to prime him before we see her not to talk about our family stuff.

❖

I don't take our personal life anywhere. In my business life I have a high degree of confidentiality, and my relationship with my wife is the same way. I don't ever, ever talk about our personal life with anybody.

It's worth remembering that you can probably never fully represent to an outsider what it's really like inside your marriage day to day.

If you're always telling the negative things and none of the good things about your spouse, it's going to affect your friends' views. My husband was sexually abused as a child, for example. There are deep things like that, things that have affected his life, that no one else is ever going to know. Outsiders can't put all of that into perspective.

I think talking to friends or family about our marriage can sometimes be an outlet, but for me there's a line. I'm a private person, so airing dirty laundry is never something I feel comfortable doing. I also don't want anyone having a negative impression of my husband, even if it's just briefly. A spouse is willing to work through a problem, compromise, and forgive, especially in minor situations. Outsiders aren't going through that process, so they may not understand when it's repaired.

I love hearing about other people's stuff, but I think it's disloyal to speak too much to others about my marriage. I can talk to my friends, and that's fine, because they won't think any less of my husband or be swayed too much. But if I start talking to family, like my sister who's been bonded to me forever, she's more likely to get a slight dislike for my husband or to be annoyed with him. I'm really careful about who I tell things to.

It's natural to compare notes on the relationship with your friends, and it can be good if you have a friend with good advice. It can go wrong, though, if you have a friend who has a sympathetic ear but then starts to feed off the negative stuff. I almost think it would be better if your friends would tell you to shut up and go get some help. Seriously, it would speed things along.

I don't like to be around women friends who are constantly husband-bashing. It's like they can't wait to get out with their girlfriends and talk about what stupid idiots they're married to. Some of these women are younger, and I think maybe they aren't at the point yet where they're adjusted. The longer they talk about their husbands this way, I think, *Right, he is a loser*, and I can't believe any of that talk is helping cure the situation.

Sometimes I get angry at my husband when he's away on business trips, and I just need to talk about it with someone to cool off. I don't have a friend like that right now, and I need one. I've actually had friends in the past who would listen to me and then judge my husband and hate him, and that doesn't help. I need someone who will listen without judgment.

I remember when we were first married, my husband and I would get together with people, and they'd gripe about their marriages. Usually it was couched in a mean sort of joke, like how the wife got in an accident because she's a terrible driver, or that the husband was so cheap that he wouldn't buy a new dishwasher when it clearly needed to be replaced. My husband and I made an agreement early on that if we have something to say, we'll say it to each other. We won't say hurtful things about each other to other people.

I have a married friend who talks to me a lot about frustrations she has with her husband, because he avoids dealing with problems and wants to pretend everything is fine all the time. Some of that venting is normal and healthy, but she brings up the same stuff all the time, and it's lasted for years. I think she says things to me that she won't say to her husband, and that seems like a problem to me.

One of the nicest things that happened to me early in my marriage was being given permission to say that I love my wife, that she's my best friend. When you're freshly minted as a married man, you get a lot of grief. At the place where I used to work, the humor was like at a high school level. Everybody was bitching about their wives, and it was brutal. One of my buddies heard the boss grumbling about his wife and said, "That sucks, man. I love my wife. My wife is great." And I thought, *Wow, that's awesome.*

My wife and I learned from a marriage workshop to always publicly say the best about each other. I've learned that if I make it a point to say only good things about her in public, it makes a great difference. If I'm standing there at the water cooler telling someone positive things like, "My wife fixed the most amazing meal last night," or "She just aced her GRE," then pretty soon, I can't wait to get home to the woman who is like *that.* But if I were to spend all my time running her down and letting other people get in on that game, my estimation of her would just drop.

At the moment I have no male colleagues. I have several work wives, so to speak, and these women like to talk. Some of them don't particularly like their present husbands, and they're quite frank about it with me.

As far as what I'll say, a little kidding and teasing about relationships is fine, and it can be humorous. I want them to know that my wife and I don't have a perfect marriage. We argue and yell, or sometimes I'm in the dog house, so I tell them that, because I think it's the kind of stuff that wouldn't be surprising. I want to defend my marriage, though. I want to respect my wife and protect her reputation.

That relationship is much more important to me than the relationship I have with my colleagues. My marriage is entitled to a higher degree of confidence.

Arguing or correcting your spouse in public can lead to a lot of hurt. (Plus, nobody likes the Bickersons.)

My first wife and I used to bicker all the time, and it became a bad habit. In fact, we even had a few arguments we'd bring out at parties to entertain our guests—arguments we thought were entertaining, like, "Was it pâté or was it cat food?" It was a part of our social repertoire, and I remember naively thinking that we sounded like we were on a sitcom, entertaining people.

Later we were in the car with my little niece, and my wife and I were just carrying on a normal conversation. Suddenly, my niece started making fun of how we were always disagreeing and going back and forth, back and forth.

I think that's when I first became conscious of what we were doing. The problem is also that this bad habit of public feuding can turn ugly. Suddenly, very personal things are being said in front of other people, and this leads to embarrassment, anger, and hurt feelings. It's about exposure. You should always be protecting your spouse, not making them vulnerable in front of others. Today, I'm sure I would be mortified if I could look back and watch how my first wife and I behaved in front of others.

I used to see my mom publicly correct my poor dad when we were growing up, and it was mortifying for him. She was mean in that way, correcting and picking at him. She'd say, "Don't eat your food that way," in a restaurant, for example. She embarrassed him. That's how I learned not to behave that way.

Under no circumstances will my husband and I ever correct each other publicly. If he's got a beef, or I've got a beef, we'll wait until we're alone to say something about it. Then, when we're in private, I'm still mad at him, but I have my dignity left. I never worry about what my husband will say in public, and I'm grateful for that.

Once, early on, I snapped at my partner in front of his friends and immediately regretted it. It was embarrassing, and it's also really bad manners. It makes people uncomfortable, and why would you want to do that? I don't like it when other people do it, so I decided I wasn't going to do it and apologized. Certain things need to be private between the two of you. That's what makes it a relationship.

We don't argue in public. If we're out with our friends, they're not going to see me get angry. I wouldn't show that. If my husband makes a tasteless joke or something, I'll give him a look but not in a way that anybody would notice.

❖

I'd never say something negative about my husband in public, and he wouldn't do it to me. I might poke good-natured fun at the fact that he's not expressive and that I'm loud and not subtle and a little off-color, but it's never done with even a modicum of malicious intent.

❖

Everybody's been in that situation where you're out with a couple and they start arguing, and you just wish you were somewhere else. Nobody wants to see that. It's uncomfortable for everybody. I figure if we can't handle our problems, why should we ask other people to be part of them?

It's worth working out the rules, because everybody needs friends.

I see some other couples who won't do anything at all unless they're with each other. One won't go to parties unless the other one goes, for example. I have a group of work-related friends, and we don't hang out with our husbands. I like having my world where I get to be independent. It's nice to have that piece of me that's still me, not just a member of a couple.

I don't think there's anything wrong with talking to my friends about my marriage. You have to account for differences between men and women because, as you know, men have no emotional needs. I'm joking, of course, but sometimes it feels like that.

My friends are, for me, and maybe for all women, extremely important. My husband has friends, but it's not the same. When I was younger, I think friends were important to help me commiserate about marriage issues. I could hear what was going on with them, and it broadened my perspective. I don't think I would have survived without that.

The friends I have tend to talk a lot about their marriages, and I enjoy listening. I don't go into great long stories like they do, and I really don't talk about my husband, but it validates some of the stuff I'm thinking. Like when someone complains about their husband wasting so many hours watching sports on TV, for example, that kind of thing makes me feel normal to hear that someone else has the same problem. Other times I hear about problems we *don't* have, and then I'm grateful that we don't.

❖

Helping you with your problems is what friends are for. The funny thing for us is that for my husband and me, it's not gender-based. He can sometimes relate to women better than men, and I sometimes talk to male friends about problems. We're not looking to resolve our disputes by talking with another person. We're talking it through. It can help to get another perspective.

❖

My wife has her girlfriends for going out on Thursday nights, and I have mine for playing golf. That's been a key for us—keeping our circle of friends and activities, not letting life change so much that they get completely blocked out. That keeps your mind healthy and sane.

❖

One of the things my wife and I didn't do when we got married was stop having friends. We kept doing what we were doing with the same circle of people we had when we were single. Having fun with our friends is one of the things that's added a lot to our married life.

❖

My wife and I do have mutual friends, but we also have a good number of friends that the other doesn't know, and we both like that. We were in the habit of doing that when we were dating. We've maintained that, and it's been helpful. You've got a little bit of yourself that the couple is not completely consuming. We see each other's independence, activities, and interests as being very important, and we allow each other to have as much of that as we can. If we were to have a marriage in which we were constantly codependent, that would push us away from each other.

My husband and I made a point of making our friends mutual friends, even our single friends. When I first met my husband, it was after a negative experience I'd had in a previous relationship, where I had friends that my boyfriend didn't get along with. That was very stressful, so the first thing I told my husband was that he was going to have to become friends with my friends. It's been great for us. We now have a group we have "family dinner" with every couple of weeks. We don't differentiate between my friends and his friends—they're all mutual friends.

My husband and I really like each other's close friends. There have been one or two exceptions along the way, but it's been very sustaining for us to have good mutual friends over the years. It's made for more compatibility and more joy. We look forward to seeing the same people. We're happy to go on vacation with them and have those people come to our home. It adds to the circle of comfort and value that's a big part of our marriage.

Chapter 6

....

CAN YOU CHANGE YOUR PARTNER?

The difficulty with marriage
is that we fall in love with a personality
but must live with a character.
—Peter De Vries

F OR SIXTEEN YEARS, my husband and I had the most awesome cairn
terrier named Nora. She was smart, funny, and affectionate,
which made her a wonderful companion—unless we were in a thunderstorm.

She wasn't like those dogs who hide in dark closets, cowering in
fear. She was just the opposite. Her approach was to stand at the window, pace, and bark at the thunder and lightning until it stopped. She
took on that storm like she was the biggest alpha wolf in the pack, and
she never gave up. The barking could go on for hours, and it was cra-
zy-making.

We even hired a dog trainer to see if he could fix it. He said that

Nora adopted this behavior because she got rewarded for it every time. She always barked at the storms, and they always eventually stopped. In her little dog brain, she thought she drove the storms away. *You're welcome.*

People have quirks and habits that can be hard to live with, too.

We complain, we're late, we eat junk food, we drive like maniacs, and all sorts of other things we could probably control but choose not to.

And as much as we all know that change needs to come from within ourselves, that doesn't stop many of us from trying to change other people. And who better than your spouse, whose habits and behavior you know better than anyone else's?

Did you marry your spouse and then try to change things about him or her? Is truly unconditional love really possible?

Our happy couples say they probably all tried to change something in their partners over the years. They also say that most of the time, it didn't work.

Yet, perspective seems to play a role in this desire to have our spouses change. As the years roll on and couples grow together, many choose to focus more on being grateful for the good and less on trying to change the things they can't control, i.e., each other.

When it comes to spouses, what you see is probably what you get.

Nothing will change your partner except age and the force of gravity.

Don't go in with the notion that you've got yourself a project. Your spouse is not a blank canvas or a lump of clay.

I used to be a divorce attorney, and people would ask me, "Why do you think people get divorced? Is it money, adultery?" I think the answer is unmet expectations. When my daughter was in preschool, she had this expression: "You get what you get, and you don't get upset." That's true in marriage. Who you get is who you get. The more you try to force change on someone, the more disappointment and resentment there is.

If someone is willing to be changed, and they see a change they want, then it's possible for something to change. But to change someone to make them the way you want them to be? No, that's a big, big, big mistake.

I think most people do try to change their partners, both men and women. I listen to other men a lot, and there's always an underlying theme of change, making people the way you want them, and that doesn't work.

My wife and I have probably changed each other more than we realize over the years, but I didn't go in thinking I needed things to change about her.

❖

My husband and I dated for about ten years before we got married because he wasn't that focused on a career. I had this idea that a guy ought to have a big bank account saved up and that he should be prepared to take on financial responsibilities and security for the sake of raising a family. I was hung up on that. I needed to think about whether the fact that he didn't have all of that was something I could be comfortable with.

I came to the conclusion that he was the one I wanted to be with no matter what, come hell or high water. I realized it didn't have to matter, but it took time to come to that conclusion.

It's just too tempting. People in happy marriages may try to change their partners, even though they know that it probably won't work.

I've found through hard experience that changing my wife is something I'm not capable of doing. She is a force of nature. She creates her own way, and efforts to divert her are wasted. With a credit card or bank account, as long as there's money, there's not much restraint on how it gets spent. I've tried to encourage her to be frugal, but it's not in her nature. She's too creative, always thinking of things we could do, and the money goes out.

I've also tried to train her to turn off lights when we're not using them in parts of the house, but I find the lights on all the time when she's outside. She just cannot think of it. It's a little bit like our dog who jumps up. No matter how many times we've told her she can't jump up on people to say hello, she forgets about it as soon as she gets excited.

My husband and I have joked since the day we got married that he's missing an aesthetic gene. He doesn't pay attention to, or care about, how he looks. He'll wear the same old clothes with moth holes in them every day. One day I dropped him off at the subway, and he went running off with his underwear hanging out of his pants. There was a big hole in the back where his wallet had worn through the pocket.

The same is true of household furnishings, rugs, and artwork. If it's still in one piece, he thinks it's good enough. He doesn't care what it looks like. None of this is a big deal, but it used to be something I tried to change, and I failed.

For years I tried to change my ex-husband. He was extremely brilliant and had all the potential in the world. I was married to potential, and I tried constantly to make that potential a reality. Of course, it never worked.

The only thing I keep trying to get my husband to change about himself is to stop smoking. I know that it's not possible for him to change for me, but it's a tough one.

I used to have a very bleak outlook on change. I thought you should assume that people don't change, but I've come to believe that people do. I've seen some changes that have occurred in my wife and some friends and family, but I also believe that you can't change another person. You can really try. You can push and push and push, and you might be successful, but I think it's hit or miss.

I don't think you can change your spouse. I found that out the hard way, because I spent years trying. Maybe small things will change, where he gives a little and says, "Okay, I'll be the one to get up and make the coffee in the morning." But for the most part he's not going to change, not in any big, fundamental way.

Oh yeah, there were things I wanted to change in my wife. We all would like to create partners in our own image, and it's a human quality to want to control the world, probably starting with your spouse, then extending to your children, then taking it out to the people you deal with. It's errant in us, in our own egos. We're at the center, and the world revolves around us. For me, my wife's strongest points, in a lot of ways, are the most difficult to deal with. It's a balancing act.

You may be able to shape each other in some ways, but you'll need to be patient. Really patient.

You can probably change a little bit in someone else, but it's part of the process of getting to know each other. And that takes years, by the way.

My husband's table manners have gotten better. He no longer takes the last dinner roll without asking if someone else wants it, and he doesn't eat food out of the pan anymore. That's progress.

I did get my husband to change some of his clothing choices. His shirts were really bad, and after a while I got up the courage to tell him I didn't like them. I think his mother picked them out.

My husband's personal hygiene was different from mine when we got together. That's definitely changed for the better.

My husband comes after me sometimes and helps me clean up my act. I might say to someone, for example, "Can I steal the salt and pepper?" rather than, "May I have…"? He'll let me know when I've worn out a phrase. He'll say, "What is this new thing you've got going on here"?

Fifteen years ago, when my wife and I got married, I thought I really needed to live in the state I grew up in. It was where I felt the happiest, but I don't feel that way anymore, so change is possible.

The changes my husband and I have made have been to better each other. I used to be a very meek person. I couldn't stand up for myself, and he taught me to believe in myself. He taught me that what I did was good. He says I've mellowed him and put reality in his life. I made him think before he jumped the gun, and he's a lot less cocky than he used to be.

My husband has taught me patience. I want everything right now or yesterday, but he's so laid back. Just observing him has helped me, and I can see that his way really works better.

I think you can shape the way you interact with each other. When we were first married, for example, I'd say something like, "How about if I do the dishes, and then could you change the oil in the car?" Every time I'd ask my husband to do something, I'd make it into "I'll do this, you do that." One day he said to me, "You can ask me to do something. You don't always have to put it in terms of 'If you do this, I'll do that.'" I didn't see it until he said so, but it was manipulative in a way.

Our marriage has made me tougher and my husband softer. They say you marry the unresolved parts of yourself, and I think the unresolved part of me did want to have a stronger part. It's happened for both of us.

When I first met my husband, I was told by friends that he was really cold. Now, years later, you can't take the guy to a violin concert with one of the kids without him turning into a big puddle of tears. I think he's always been emotional, but he feels free to show his emotions now more than he used to.

❖

When our kids were young, my husband didn't help me out very much. Now he'll often say, "Can I help you with something?" or, "Let me do that for you." He never used to do that. He's a lot more thoughtful of me today than he was earlier on. I appreciate when he gets my car started and turns my seat heater on before I get in when it's cold. He does lots of little things now, and it's pretty nice.

For years, I felt like when my wife was in the embrace of her family, she was a different person. She would immediately assume a role like she had in her childhood. I didn't find it endearing, and I talked to her about it a couple of times. That's such a powerful pull for any person, and her family, in particular, is a collection of really strong personalities.

For years, anytime we'd go there, I'd be sweating bullets. I was never comfortable, but it's changed. My wife broke a lot of her patterns, and we have a really good time with her family now. Twenty years ago, I'd never have predicted that.

Leading by example works with your kids, at least some of the time. It can also work with your spouse.

On occasion my husband and I might not agree on something, or he might not conform to what I think is the proper way of handling a situation. But sitting there bitching at him is certainly not going to get him to change. You can only lead by example.

I've become more compassionate than I was before I met my wife. Once, when she and I were first dating, we were going back to my place, and I lived downtown. I was pulling into the underground parking garage, and there was this drunk guy right in the driveway. I drove around him, and she was mortified.

When we were out together, she'd take her leftovers and give them to homeless people on the street. That was one of the differences between her and me, so I've gotten more sensitive to some of that because of her influence. With the guy in my driveway, she thought I should have stopped to see if he was okay. Without her, I'd still be tempted to drive around him.

My husband has very high moral standards, higher than my own. One Christmas we decided to travel to Canada. We had three hams in the freezer, so I stuck one in the suitcase to take with us. We got to customs and they said, "Do you have anything to declare?" Naturally, I was just going to smuggle it through, but my husband said, "We have a ham!" I'm hoping that someday, I'll be as good as he is and can turn over a new leaf. He really is a better person than I am, and I love that he loves me anyway.

❖

My wife's a habitual list-maker, and I've become one—but I don't know whether that's because of her influence or my old age.

❖

My husband taught me how to say no to things. He told me I don't have to explain myself, which I used to do. You can just say no. It wasn't a lack of confidence, but he said, "Why say so much when you don't have to?"

❖

My husband has made changes, and I see that as a gift. He's done really brave things and accomplished so much, but it's not because I said he needed to. I look at women who say things to their husbands like, "Why didn't you do this? You should do this." That's not my style at all. With me, it's like, if you want to come along for the ride with me, then come along for the ride. This is who I am. I think that resonates with your partner after a while.

I remember watching my husband at the grocery store one time, and he makes conversation with everybody. I thought, *I want to do that.* There are parts of his personality I try to emulate. It sounds cheesy, but I think I'll be a better person when I can be more like him.

What I've realized is that when I encourage my husband in the simplest way by saying, "I like that shirt on you," or, "Thank you for picking up the kids at the bus today," it makes a huge difference. When I show him even the tiniest amount of appreciation, he starts saying those kinds of things back to me, and it really makes me feel good. It makes it a better day. The more I approach it this way, the more he rises to the occasion.

Part of what works for my husband and me is to keep appreciating each other's gifts and talents and allowing the other person to continue to grow. It's surprising how much we change over time. I always thought I'd get to a point and be the same person, but I've changed significantly since I met my husband, and part of that is just due to his influence.

I'm not that nice to people sometimes, but I'm consciously trying to change that based on my husband's good example. He doesn't overreact; he doesn't bite people's heads off. You can retrain yourself to deal with those impulses, and that's what being with him has done for me.

Happy couples work to accept each other's behavior. This is an ongoing effort, one that never ends.

My wife wanted a third dog, and I really didn't. We went to the mall together, and she went into a pet store and saw this cute little dog. I was getting a haircut, and she came and said, "We're going to go look at this dog. We're just going to look." So, what am I going to do? Of course, we got the dog, and he's just a terror. He makes life so stressful. It was a big mistake, and she admits now that it was a mistake, too.

I'd rather we had a lot less TV watching in our house, but my wife likes to watch TV. I realized that, for the most part, it's just not worth fighting about. I figure, what's the point? I'm not going to change that.

I've had to adjust to the speed with which my wife likes to do things. She makes a decision and goes zero to 60 immediately, and in my mind, she's not thinking of all the stuff that needs to happen in between. Last night we were talking about a renovation to our house. She thinks we can do it all in a weekend, and I'm like, "This is a five-week job!" Well, when she hears it's a five-week job, she doesn't want to do it anymore. She throws up her hands.

The best decision I made in our marriage was to accept my husband the way he was. I welcomed his friends when they came. I could never imagine making him change his friends or his habits just because I didn't like them. Part of the commitment is accepting your spouse as they are, warts and all. You accept them, and that's how you're going to live with them.

You don't have to change. You don't have to be molded, but allow yourself to adapt. Just try to get through that particular moment where you might say, "I really don't want to do this. I don't like the fact that she does that." It doesn't matter; just let it happen. It's usually only going to last for five, ten minutes. That's all it is, and it's not difficult.

I've given the book *Men Are from Mars, Women Are from Venus* to so many friends in so many different languages. That book opened my eyes. In my work as a cross-cultural consultant, I almost see the man/woman thing as a cultural difference. You become tolerant when you understand that the other person has a different perception of things. To work it out, you become a translator.

❖

My husband and I are very, very different. We've gone through crises and tough stuff, and that's really when the differences come out. The moment I let go of expecting him to be a certain way, the better our marriage got.

It might be worthwhile to change your own behavior if it helps the marriage.

Only babies are allowed to act any way they feel like acting all the time. In a marriage, both people have to make an effort to be their best, not their worst.

One of the lessons I have been learning, slowly but surely, is that real love is action. It's not just a feeling, and it's not just saying, "I love you." I've learned that with my wife, if I *do* something, it means so much more to her. Once I started becoming truly conscious of it, I've learned new habits. For example, she usually gets up first in the mornings, so I started to make the bed every day, and it really pleased her. My mother didn't teach me that, and neither did my first wife. I still usually don't feel like making the bed, but now I can't leave the room without doing it.

Whether you're consciously thinking about it or not, everyone has expectations for their relationship, for their spouse. When those expectations aren't fulfilled, you feel disappointment. You can make an effort to live up to the expectations your spouse has for you—or you say can no, I'm not interested. But you have to realize that when people have disappointment after disappointment after disappointment, it adds up. People's thresholds for happiness differ, and you have to recognize what your spouse's expectations are and decide whether you're willing to give a little.

I know I'm hard, and my wife and friends tell me I'm hard, and that's just me. I'm not the most emotive person because I didn't grow up with it. I'm not a verbal person, so talking makes me uncomfortable. I come from a dysfunctional family where I saw fighting, physical abuse, and verbal abuse. I don't love those qualities about myself, though, and I think people change if they want to change. I've learned patience the hard way, and I think I'm doing a good job. I have to count to ten or one hundred a lot, so the change that you want isn't easy. It requires a lot of work, and you've got to want it.

A man basically needs beer and a place to sleep, and he's happy. A woman is much more complicated and has many more needs. I've learned how important it is for my wife to feel that she's totally consumed with my attention—that she knows I love her, that there is nothing in this world I wouldn't do for her, that I adore her. I know this is important to her, but not only that; when I exhibit those emotions to her, it adds to my value.

I've struggled all my life with attention span and forgetfulness. I get zeroed in on something and forget everything else. Early in our marriage my wife would ask me to do things, and I'd forget, and we fought about it several times. She challenged me to take responsibility for things, not to accept this trait but instead to work on changing it, and I did.

Now when she asks me to do something that's going to be a challenge for me to remember, I know to build in more coping mechanisms. I'll make notes to myself or send myself an email or set my watch alarm to go off in the middle of the day so that something will interrupt me and remind me that I need to do it. I wasn't prioritizing or being diligent about remembering things early in our marriage. After we went around that track several times, I learned that it was important.

I had notions of changing my husband through the years. When our kids were young, he was away at work every day and several nights a week. When he came home, he just wanted to sit down and read the paper. I think I felt a little used because I had the kids from morning to night, until they got to bed while he was out working during the day. I had to learn to live with that, and it turns out I changed myself.

Through my spiritual life I found out I had a right to be the way I was, and he had a right to be the way he was. That improved things.

All through my dating life, I had a bad habit of playing games in my relationships. Whether they were good men or bad men, it didn't matter. I'd create fights to cause a breakup, just to see if they would come back. It was very immature behavior.

A few months after I started dating my husband, I did that with him. I knew he was a wonderful person, but I picked a fight with him, and I dumped him. There was no reason; I was just playing a game. Luckily, he stuck around, and within two weeks we were back together. After that, though, he said to me, "Don't ever do that again, because I won't come back next time." I knew immediately I could never play that game again, and I've never done it since.

People can change, but only if they have some sort of conflict or experience that is so profound it makes them change themselves. You might bring out the best in someone for a while, even for an ongoing period, but that's not changing the person's basic personality makeup, or how a person really is. Change is a spiritual thing that has to come from within, and it can't come from another person.

In one sense, I've changed my behavior a lot because of the way that my husband is. I had to learn to be careful with him because he's sensitive, so I've learned to control my tone. You need to be sensitive to people's backgrounds and their soft spots. The last thing I want to do is hurt his feelings unintentionally, for no reason.

I think how you change each other is by a sort of osmosis. When I met my husband, I wanted to be a better person for him. Any of the things I didn't like about myself, and they weren't the nicest things in the world, I wanted to change for him because I saw him as such a good human being. To me, that's a healthy way for a person to change you in a marriage.

One thing that's changed for my wife and me is PDA, public displays of affection. I was raised in a family that didn't do that at all. We had a lot of love for each other but didn't show it by touching or holding hands or kissing someone in public. All of those physical affirmations of care and love are things that mean a lot to my wife, and she told me that it meant something to her. It was hurtful to her when I refused to do it, so I made a significant effort for a long time. If we were sitting together, I'd put my arm around her shoulder or rub her back, and if we were walking, we'd hold hands or I'd give her a kiss in public. It was very uncomfortable at first, but now it's actually second nature.

In a marriage you have to think about the effects of your actions. There was nothing right, or inherently appropriate, about my prudishness. It was hurtful to my wife to act the way I'd been acting, so I was intentional about trying to change.

I think sometimes there's a misperception that what people do is somehow genetic, like, "That's just the way I am." We always heard, "Well, that's the way Grandpa Joe was." Well, that doesn't excuse that Grandpa Joe was a jackass. That doesn't make it all right. If you have some quirk about you that's not nice, why wouldn't you try to change yourself to make your marriage work better?

Chapter 7

....

THE BIG INGREDIENTS: TIME AND TALK

Chains do not hold a marriage together.
It's threads, hundreds of tiny threads,
which sew people together through the years.
—Simone Signoret

R EMEMBER THAT PHRASE, the "work of marriage"? It's been an undercurrent of everything discussed so far, but here I'd like to wave a flag and say that this chapter is all about the "work of marriage" and how happy couples do it.

According to those interviewed, time and talk emerged as the most fundamental elements in what is commonly referred to as the "work of marriage."

Talk is real, soul-baring communication that helps you learn about yourself, your spouse, and who you are together. It's about telling the truth, even when you're afraid the other person might not like it, and it definitely carries the potential for an occasional ugly cry.

Time is the other element. It doesn't matter who you are—time is available only in limited quantities. Time, in the "work of marriage," is making the choice to spend time with your spouse. It's valuing the marriage over doing other things you occasionally really want to do. Typically, it also means the TV needs to be turned off, so it's a pretty serious choice.

How do happy couples get the most out of both talk and time? It's a process. It takes practice. It changes from year to year, and it never ends.

The payoff, however, is huge. Time and talk create compatibility, and when compatibility is present in a marriage, everything else seems to run more smoothly.

Talk, talk, and talk some more.
Then get up tomorrow and do it again.

Intimate conversation is the glue that binds two people. It creates a bond like no other.

My husband and I had to learn to communicate. I remember being really mad once early in our marriage. He didn't come home for dinner because he was at a used book sale. We had a baby, and I had to leave for something at seven in the evening, and he got home right before seven when we normally ate at six.

He didn't understand why that was a problem. I was mad at the fact that I had dinner ready and was waiting. It was okay that he bought books, but I felt like it was insensitive and selfish that he didn't think it was important to let me know he'd be late. Figuring out all the nuances of this episode took a long time for us both to understand.

I guess I thought that my husband was supposed to read my mind. I think women expect that men will learn all these things about them, and eventually we'll have to communicate less. I've realized that's not true.

If you don't talk, that's when things go wrong. That's when something can happen that you don't like. You can have an argument about something because you might have spoken to one another about general things, but you're not properly talking. You need to talk about real things with each other all the time.

My husband and I still have to work at communication. He doesn't like to sit down and hash things out because his parents fought a lot when he was growing up. Now he just wants everything to be okay, but it's like he wants peace at any price. That's artificial, and he sometimes wants to pretend the issues aren't there so we don't get into an argument. I literally have to say, "We're going to sit down and have a talk like two adults. We don't need to fight, but we need to talk." And you can almost see it in his face: *I don't want to do this*. It's a struggle sometimes.

There's a difference between men and women when it comes to talking about the relationship. Men see it as risk, while women see it as discovery and opportunity. The hardest thing in the world is to get me to answer questions about the "us." I'm serious. My wife has three of those stupid books where they ask questions like, "If you were locked in an elevator with a supermodel, who would it be?" She wants to do these exercises all the time, and at first, I really hated it. My wife saw it as an opportunity to learn more about each other, and I saw it as, *Wow, I'm really going to get into trouble when I answer the supermodel question*. I'll answer, and then she'll say, "Oh, so you like blondes?" Ultimately, it's been good to deal with a lot of the questions, but men and women see this process very differently.

Marriage is a learning experience, and you learn a lot of things quickly. You learn things about your spouse, and you learn what kind of reaction you'll get to certain things. Then you make the decision to do something or not, depending on where you want to end up.

After forty years, my husband can't keep anything from me. I'll look at his face and say, "You're not telling me everything," or I'll see that he doesn't agree with something I just said.

You really do have to talk about things every day. A tough part of it for us now is when my husband comes home from work. I'm so anxious to talk to him, but he's just anxious to get behind the bar and fix himself a drink. I'm going, "Blah blah blah," and he's not listening. I still need to learn to stop and let him calm down before I bring up the topics of the day.

My husband and I require a lot of air time together, just a lot of talk time. If you talk and share everything, then when you come up against something difficult, it's easier because you know each other so well.

Email has been a great way for my husband and me to communicate. I'm not the best communicator verbally, but I'm really good with email. It's easier for me to write than it is to talk. When it comes to planning and decisions, I function so much better in writing. When my husband and I realized that certain things are best communicated this way, that made a big difference. The caveat to this is pure emotion: that doesn't work in an email.

I love talking about our marriage. I told my husband I'd love to go to counseling just for fun. I've gotten him to do a lot of things to examine the relationship, like reading books or doing certain activities together. He doesn't want to admit it, but he knows these things have been good for us.

Texting works really well for my wife and me. We probably send twenty or thirty texts to each other throughout the day when we're both at work. She lets me know how our daughter did after she drops her off at daycare, tells me about interesting things that go on during the day, or we talk about finances and what we need to spend. It helps us stay on the same page. We make sure we're both facing the same direction at the same time.

My husband listens less now than he used to. You sometimes tend to tune out your partner as you progress in your relationship. Unless you work on it, you tend to do things that could hurt your marriage if you're not careful, like tuning them out, disrespecting them, speaking badly. Those are the things you need to constantly work on in your marriage.

One of the reasons I fell in love with my wife is that I just loved talking with her. She's a great conversationalist, she's a good listener, and she has interesting ideas. We never seem to run out of conversation, even after twenty-six years. It's one of the things that keeps our marriage very strong: we talk, talk, talk all the time. I come home from work, and I'm in the kitchen and we're talking, then we go upstairs and talk some more, then we go for a walk and talk some more. There's a lot that we say, and there's not a lot that we have to wonder about.

❖

When we were dating and trying to figure out our relationship, we decided to take a long weekend and rent a cabin away from the city where we could have complete solitude. My husband brought two identical books called *All About Me* that had all these pointed questions you needed to fill out about existential issues, love, life, first experiences, and that kind of thing. We spent part of the weekend filling out the books, and then we exchanged them and read what the other person wrote. It's worth it to make a deliberate effort to understand each other. That weekend we decided we loved each other, and we made that the date of our anniversary.

My husband and I are both very analytic and very intentional. I studied marriage counseling and worked in it for a short time. If he ever did anything that I thought was scary, I'd say "Red flag, red flag!" I knew the communication patterns to avoid, and I'd say, "You're invalidating me," or "That's one of [marriage expert] John Gottman's Four Horses of the Apocalypse for Relationships!" It was all a bit much, but it provided a lot of comic relief.

Truth or dare?
Telling the truth about yourself is essential.

When my wife and I were dating, I made a point of vomiting the truth of who I was all over her—what I believed, how I thought about things, all the mistakes I'd made, every single secret I could think of. It wasn't pretty. I suppose my thought was, *If we're going to have a relationship, then let's not waste time discovering these things ten years from now. I'm going to be truthful with you now so that I can always be truthful with you later.*

I didn't want to be any less than myself. If you can't risk exposing your real heart to your spouse, then what's the point?

I had a bad relationship in my past, and over a period of time I closed off until there was nothing much left. I didn't reveal myself and became very defensive about things. I learned to be closed up for self-protection. After that relationship ended, I lived alone for a while, and I was very happy with that. And when my current relationship started, I was determined not to make the same mistakes again. I simply decided to be myself. That was new, and it's exhilarating.

The outcome needs to meet the expectations in a marriage, or you have to try as best you can. If you can work hard to communicate where you are today and what your expectations are from the other person, you can both work toward the outcome. If the outcome is worse than the expectations, then you're going to fight and be depressed and miserable. But if the outcome is better than the expectations, like it often is for my wife and me, that's when you're living in glee and happiness.

In our marriage, I probably say to my wife most of the things that come into my head. It can get me into trouble, but we don't hold our tongues. We're proactive about communicating, and we don't hold stuff back. We don't say belligerent things, but we'll argue. We actually kind of enjoy fighting it out.

To me, the whole point of marriage is to help each other become better selves. The best communication I've had with my wife is the most vulnerable, down-to-the-bone communication you could possibly think of. Whether it's about something painful, distasteful, or one of those "if my parents ever heard me saying this it would break their hearts" kind of talks, those conversations have brought us closer to each other.

Men and women are different, and my husband and I, in particular, are very different from each other. When he gets angry, for example, I learned that the best approach is not to say, "We need to talk about this," but rather, "Don't talk to me like that." I've learned that he needs to be angry sometimes. A woman wouldn't want that, but you have to read the other person's personality and sensibility and know where they're coming from. It's not about how you'd react. It took years for me to learn that about him—years, years, years.

It's very strange, because I'm like a lot of women in that no matter who we are, we're uncomfortable with ourselves. I used to wonder, *Is he going to love me, is he going to like me, is he going to think I'm smart?* When my husband and I first got together, we'd gone out on maybe four dates. We were sitting in this restaurant talking—just talking, that was the amazing thing to me—and mid-sentence he said, "I love you." And it took my breath away. For him to have said that so early in our relationship, I didn't know what to say. That night he went to my house, and he never went home. It's the first time I've ever been my-self in a relationship. It's exciting, and there's something about it that frees you.

In every relationship I had before I met my wife, it always imploded after about six or eight months. They say that when you're dating, you're with the person's representative or their agent. You're afraid to show your true colors. My wife was the first person who really accept-ed me from the beginning.

I needed to be real with my husband from the start, and I think we've done a pretty good job about being completely honest. I know that no matter how I act, how neurotic I am, he'll still accept me at the end of the day. It's a relief. It takes a lot of effort not to be yourself.

With our whole group of friends, there are so many things they don't know about me that you could fill the Grand Canyon with them. My wife knows everything, and that's what you want. She's the only person I've never kept a secret from. You want someone who knows the worst qualities about you and thinks that it's okay, that you're still a great person.

It's a foreign concept to me to think there is something I can't tell my wife. Not that you ever want to lie to your spouse, but I've never been able to successfully lie to her. We've come to the realization that there's nothing either one of us can keep, or needs to keep, from the other.

At the end of the day, you have to understand what your individual goals and aspirations are. People continue to evolve and change at different ages, but at the same time, do you have the same plan? It's going to get altered, but are you trying to get to the same point together? In some of our friends' marriages that have broken up, we've seen that the partners didn't communicate the ways they were changing as individuals. If you don't communicate what's happening inside yourself, it can spawn a lot of grudges and resentment.

Before my husband and I decided to get engaged, we sat down together and had what we call our Business Deal. I come from a divorced family; both my parents are divorced several times over, so it was important to me to make sure we weren't just acting on a feeling. I wanted to know that the marriage would really work out. We hashed out how we felt about kids, school, jobs, church, and lifestyle. We were each brutally honest about who we were, what we wanted, what our goals were, and how we wanted to live together. I won't say there was negotiating, but we really wanted to make sure that we could live together. That was the framework. Some of the things we discussed originally have changed, but we knew what our starting point was.

Date night: some do, some don't. The point is to make time for each other, away from the kids if you have them.

For the last twelve years, my wife and I have had a date night on Wednesdays. It's just as exciting to me now as when we started. If I'm at work on a Wednesday, I'll really look forward to going out with her at night. Or on the weekends I'll be out with the guys playing golf, and I'll think, *I miss my wife and kids.* You see all these people who are running around trying to find someplace to be other than at home, and I don't feel that way. When the weekend comes and I'm with my family, there's no place in the world I'd rather be.

It takes effort to know each other and continue that process. We find an activity outside of our kids and date each other every single week. We've been playing kickball for the last few seasons in a league. After this is done, we'll find something like a painting or clay modeling class. I don't think we've ever felt like it was forced. We both look forward to it so much.

Every Sunday evening for years now my husband has made dinner for the two of us. I always look forward to that, because once Sunday night rolls around, I'm off duty as a mom. I read the paper and have a glass of wine. He makes the dinner and cleans it up. The value of that dinner has been huge. I so look forward to that time together.

My wife and I have a standing date night on Fridays. We've been intentional about that for years. We might share date night with very good friends, but we don't do anything that feels like work or a professional obligation.

It's good for couples to get into whatever rhythm they can to have this regular time. I still have a sense of expectation and excitement about it. I can push on through to the end of the week and look forward to that night when I can have dinner out with my wife. The idea of having dinner with her is exciting to me. I really like that girl.

We'll go away sometimes for a couple days to a B&B to have reconnect time. There have been times where I'm working every night and every weekend for two or three weeks because I'm trying to get a proposal in, and then my husband will say to me, "We need a date night," so we'll do it then. But when we're seeing enough of each other, to say that Thursday night is the night we're going to go out to dinner— whether you want to or not, whether you have a headache or not—it's unproductive for us.

❖

You're still individuals, even though you're married. You're not only dealing with your own problems, you're working on the other person's as well. When you combine that with everyday life, talking to each other can get passed over. We put our romantic night in our Outlook calendar. It sounds funny that the phone alarm will go off to remind us at eight at night, this is just the reality of making it happen.

Vacation time is valuable.

My husband and I had some problems in our marriage a while back. It was a temporary thing, but it was a nudge that you have to keep your eye on each other. You need to be careful not to get too bogged down in your own world. You have to reconnect and talk. If you don't make time for it, you can just go along on your treadmill for months and months, hardly talking because life keeps you so busy. I do almost think there should be one night a month where you get away from home, and not necessarily in a public place, because then sometimes you can't talk properly. A long car ride is good because you're stuck together. There's nobody else there, no distractions, and gradually the things you need to talk about will come out.

If everyone could live in a bubble, I bet a lot of couples' conflicts would be gone. Everyone gets so busy, though, and that's why vacations are really important to my husband and me. We have time to talk that we don't have in the usual run of things. You have to make a point of talking every day, not just coming home from work and watching TV.

My husband and I go to Paris every year on our anniversary. It's kind of like a summit. It's our special time to really focus on each other, to have some of the strategic conversations we need to have about our marriage and our life and our next steps. We stay in the same hotel every time so we're not under this intense pressure to discover more than one new thing a day. We make room in the vacation for actually being with each other, not being in the place. It's the highlight of our year, and we have some of our best conversations. This is not to say we go there and don't have arguments. Sometimes we'll spend part of the day arguing and part of the day making up, but we're having conversations that need to be had.

Having big decisions and conversations about life-altering things like having a baby in the day-to-day of my life, I don't feel like I can really think and know my own mind. Even if we've taken a one-hour dinner to talk about it, my response would inevitably be, "Well, I just don't know."

When my husband and I go away together, that's time for me specifically to really focus on decisions that need to be made. Without it, my approach is typically so moment-to-moment that the big decisions are precisely the type of thing I'd put off until tomorrow.

My vacation with my wife every year is like an off-site retreat. It's a morale event. We'll bring issues to the table and create a little agenda, a working list of goals we discuss loosely. It's not super formal, but we do try to write out what we want to talk about. Sometimes we talk about planning for big expenditures. These are discussions of priorities, how we spend our time and our money. We have a great time, and I feel like we need to do even more of it: more off-sites, more planning, more follow-up, more brainstorms, more whiteboarding.

Staying close will take extra effort for couples who spend a lot of time apart.

Being apart has gotten harder instead of easier over the years. My husband works away, and I work, too, so I'm pretty busy. I'm not as free to go be with him if there's something special or we just really feel like we need to be together. It's also been hard on him because he has some issues with sleep. He has really rough nights and has to get up and go to work. I feel terrible because I'm not around to help him with that.

When we're apart, I worry about how my wife is handling all her responsibilities. She's under a lot of stress and running from one thing to another. I try to make sure I talk to her once at night and sometime during the day, too, just to see how she's doing.

I work away from home during the week, and it's gotten increasingly difficult for my wife and me to manage. We're trying to keep up via phone, but sometimes one of us feels like talking and the other person doesn't. Still, we manage to talk, even briefly, a couple times a day just to keep up with each other. It takes effort.

When my wife worked away from home, she'd come home on the weekends and we'd get into disagreements because I'd had to make decisions without her. Then we found out that texting really helped us out. We started to text about little household things. It really helped to be able to tell her that I'd just received an estimate to have some work done in the house, for example, or if a question came up about the dog.

Being able to talk even briefly about decisions that affected us both helped us have fewer unpleasant surprises when she came home. It also gave her the opportunity to say, "Do whatever you think is best." Because she'd been given the option to weigh in, I think it made it easier for her to accept the way I did things or made the choices I did.

My husband is out of town a lot, so when he's home, we make a point of being with each other. We've never done girls' or guys' night out. For the last forty years, any activity we've ever had, we've done together.

My wife worked out of state for almost two years, and I put as much technology into it as possible. We video chatted and texted all the time. Sometimes I'd even send her regular mail, little love notes or pictures, that she could actually pick up in her mailbox at her apartment. I sent her flowers at the office from time to time.

We also made a point of talking every night, even if it was just for five minutes, and I always wanted to know when she was in safely for the evening so I wouldn't worry about her being out by herself.

We made a big effort to know what the other person was doing every single day and provide help or encouragement. It's really important to stay relevant in each other's lives; if you become irrelevant to each other, that's when it's easy to drift apart.

Believe it or not, some happy couples say they prefer each other's company to anyone else's in the world.

I hear so many guys saying, "I can't wait to go play golf so I can get away from my wife," always looking to get away. My wife and I have never felt that way about each other. We look forward to weekend mornings when we can go to Home Depot, buy plants, pick up fertilizer, work together in the yard, go places. We love going out and doing things together as a team.

My wife is my best friend. I've never really wanted to spend a lot of time out with the guys. Guys' night out has no appeal to me. I enjoy being with her, though she thinks maybe I should get out more. I don't. I'm content.

My husband and I prefer each other's company. It sounds so boring, but we really have a great time together. We've never thought we should take separate vacations for the health of our marriage, for example. We'd rather be together.

One of the things that's really held my wife and me together for forty years is that we've always done a lot of things together. I've never taken off without her on a Saturday morning to play golf while she goes out and does her own thing. We spend our free time together. We've trained dogs, raised our kids through soccer and football and cheerleading. Doing things together is really important for our marriage.

I'd much rather go out to dinner with my wife, just the two of us, than with friends. When you go out, you can talk and catch up. You don't do that when you're at home and running around. We don't have kids at home anymore, and it's not that we have these tremendous events going on, but the point is that you go out and sit down together and talk. We do that a lot, and it's probably the most enjoyable time I have, just with the two of us.

Some people have insecurity about the fact that every moment of their marriage isn't like a butterfly-in-love type of moment. But this is a long, sustained marriage, and of all the people in my life, my wife is the one I like talking to the most.

Chapter 8

....

WHAT ROMANCE?

Marriage changes passion.
Suddenly you're in bed with a relative.
—Author Unknown

L OVE, LUST, SEX, ROMANCE, PASSION: let the jokes begin. Is marriage
the death of all of them? To hear some people tell it, yes.

But the happy couples interviewed say no. Or at least...not entirely.
I mean, it depends. Did I just have a big, heavy meal, and how late at
night are we talking about?

Romance in marriage can't be boiled down to easy answers, but it
definitely still exists.

Like every other activity, sex takes a little more effort as people
age. And it might not look exactly the way it did when you were
young. But where there's a will and partners still have attraction for
each other, then love will do a double shot of espresso and find a way.

It's also a reciprocal activity where both people need to feel loved
and fulfilled. Getting it right every single time for both people involved is probably wishful thinking.

So, what kind of romantic effort is needed in a marriage long-term? How do two people come to agree on how often romantic moments are necessary, or even if they're necessary at all?

And as the years roll on, are sex and romance still important?

The consensus in our interview group is that happy marriages are complex unions that are defined by much more than sex. Romance is one ingredient, not the whole recipe—though when it's present, the dish is definitely tastier and more satisfying.

Bon appetit!

Hormones are tricky little taskmasters. Like everything else, sex can change as the years pass.

It takes a while for partners to get along really well in the intimate part of married life. I once asked my dad for some advice in that area. He said it was like one of those old radios with the big knob that tuned in the stations. You move it to the left, then to the right, then back again, and eventually you tune in to the right frequency.

I remember having some misconceptions about what married life was going to be like in terms of sexual intimacy and how frequently that would occur with my wife. I grew up in a house full of boys, and I think I grew up with this American myth that being married is a license to have all the sex you want. The problem is that there are two of you, and you're not always in agreement. Your spouse is saying, "Oh, yes, all the sex I want," and you're saying, "All the sex I want," and it's not always the same. That took some time for me to adjust to.

I came from a college environment where a lot of guys thought you had to trick women into sex because they didn't really enjoy it. I knew a lot of guys who believed this, but now I know better. With my wife, our love life is very reciprocal, and she enjoys it a lot. We both take care of ourselves and are careful about how we present ourselves to each other, and we both work to find ways to make each other crazy occasionally.

My husband and I have made it clear to each other that we're willing to try anything once. I've known a lot of people who cheated on their spouses, and sex has been the biggest reason they did so. They weren't getting what they needed at home. A lot of people can't even talk about this, but it's really important to us. We've explored a lot of things, and we're comfortable with that. Neither of us needs to indulge in fantasies we can't talk about or wonder what something would be like. It's funny, because once we opened the door to trying anything, we found we're most comfortable just being with each other. We come back to what most people would call normal.

Dating and marriage are different. When you're dating, it's more sexual, and everything is a new experience. Marriage is a much deeper, bigger thing. The challenge now is for my wife and me to create more of the dating-type moments, the things we did before, because those were really good moments.

My husband and I work really hard on being honest with each other about what's attractive to us. We work on what's appealing to the other person. My husband, for example, really finds me attractive when I've just gotten home from a workout and have no makeup or deodorant on. I used to never want him to touch me if I was dirty, but I've learned to compromise on that because it's something he really likes. I used to really like lace and coming out of the shower clean and fresh, but that doesn't do it for him. Honesty is key to keeping the sexual part of our relationship healthy.

Sometimes keeping the romance going means you need to act, then trust that the feeling will follow. I can say this with certainty from personal experience with my wife. You sometimes need to make a lot of effort when you don't feel like it or when you're tired.

It seems unromantic to talk about it, but let's say you come home on a Friday night, you're tired, your career is under the gun, and you don't feel like going out for dinner. If you say, well, it's not just going out for dinner. We'll go to a place with a little ambience, and we'll have a chance to talk and then walk in the park. That's the kind of extra effort, because you don't feel like it at the time. Then the next day you're thinking, "Yeah, I'm glad I did that," and you act a little differently toward your wife, and it makes it that much easier the next time.

I love my wife, and I'm attracted to her, but romance isn't one of our strong suits. She's romantic in things she does for me, like with gifts or making me wonderful dinners. Those things mean a lot to me. But if romance involves sexual behavior, then truthfully, I wish there were more.

Our sex life has only gotten better with marriage, but my wife and I had the opposite problem of a lot of couples. She wanted to have sex all the time, and I didn't want it as much. Our friends laugh at us, because it's the opposite of what you usually think of. We had to talk about slowing it down, spacing it out. I just couldn't do it as much as she wanted. Now that we have kids, she's okay that we've slowed it down. She says she doesn't have the feelings quite so strongly every day when I walk in the door.

Sex is hard to sustain over a length of time. You have to keep thinking of ways to make it more interesting. It doesn't have the same appeal it did when you first met. It's nothing more than that.

I reject relationship experts who tell you how you should be getting along and how much sex you should be having. I wouldn't put much stock in what someone else says about how much sex we should be having to have a healthy relationship. My wife and I are on the same page. Sex is not something either of us has to force. We are intimate when we want to be intimate. We go through times when we're having sex as much as possible, and then there may be a period where weeks go by without it, and that works for us. My experience tells me you have to go with your instincts on things. I reject the notion that you need to have a certain amount of sex, or that you should be having a date every week or working with some other person's formula for a successful relationship.

I think some people base the security of their marriage on whether they're having sex once or twice a week. But for my wife and me, there are a lot of other things under the romance umbrella. It could be just having dinner and then talking a walk together. It's a lot of different acts and gestures. Sex is this barometer people use when they're dating, but life throws so much more at you in a marriage that I think you have to take a cumulative measure of romance as you go along.

My husband is far more disciplined than I am, and as a result, I'm fatter than he is. My hair's turned grey. I don't feel terribly seductive, and I don't think I'm going to be prancing around in a two-piece bathing suit anytime soon. I feel wistful about that, and there are days that it does make me sad, because I'm sure both of us would give anything to go back and feel like having sex three times a day. It's all part of the aging process, and it's one of the doors that closes as you get older. We do have romance in our lives, but it's smaller and has more to do with loving than lusting.

❖

My wife and I still have romantic evenings, but after twenty-seven years of marriage, they're fewer and farther between. We're busier than ever, so it's harder to find time. Hormonal situations change in both men and women, too, making it less urgent than it used to be. We find ourselves often just falling into bed exhausted at the end of the day. We're under a lot of stress right now between life and work. None of this sets off alarm bells—but I will say I'm not all that happy with it, either.

Aging is affecting both my husband and me. I don't spend a lot of time worrying about it, but I do think about managing it as I go through menopause. I've been on hormones and off hormones and back on them, trying to get myself settled, having nothing to do with sex but with anxiety attacks and night sweats and all that stuff. My husband's suffering now from bouts of insomnia, so the few times we do have sex, he winds up staying awake all night looking at the ceiling thinking, "Why did I do that?" The idea of going to bed, having a good romp, and then sleeping it off has become much more complicated than it used to be.

Spring for the babysitter.
Alone time helps keep the spark.

We have a babysitter booked every Saturday night, even if we don't have plans. Sometimes we get in the car and it's like, "Well, what are we doing?"

Getaways really help my wife and me, but our ability to get away is very, very limited. We're just after that sense of being able to relax or have a conversation without a schedule. So many things in our house now have a five-minute time limit on them before one of the kids throws something through a window. When we can do it, we do, and we actually work very hard at finding opportunities to get away.

For me, the question isn't what marriage does to romance—it's what having children does to it. Everything changes. This is especially true for women, because our energy is geared toward the children. Not that men's energy isn't, but I know that at the end of the day, I'm just done. I'm spent. It's very tough to get back in gear sometimes. My husband and I really try to get away together. We have to physically get away and spend time with each other. If we didn't make the effort, I really think I'd be in bed by nine every night, even on weekends.

Some of the most romantic times I have with my wife are when we go to a bar and sit down and just have a drink together. That's really romantic to me, because we're being man and woman, and we're outside of our house and all the chores and stresses that come with it. It also reminds me of times when we had our first drinks together in other places. For some reason, it's important to get out of the house.

My wife and I have really worked on our romantic life over the years. There's no problem in that area that time and rest and privacy can't cure. And if you can get away from your kids for a long weekend in a remote place, it makes a big difference.

I like the feeling of no responsibilities whatsoever kid-wise or the freedom to talk about things that don't even matter, gossiping about other people, just silly stuff my husband and I don't typically have time for. We're after pretty simple pleasures. We may just go out to a restaurant nearby and sit and be boring with each other. If you put a drink in front of us and just leave us alone, we're good to go.

Is "I love you" a magic phrase? Some say yes, some say no.

We say we love each other every day, which I think is important. Some people say it's just words, but it's not. When you're going through tough times, you need to hear that. You need to have that daily kiss, that daily hug. You have that moment where you just drink in the other person for like thirty seconds, and then everything else is fine. Having affection for each other every day is a critical component of staying married.

❖

I remember when my husband and I were first married, we used to leave love notes on Post-its around the house for each other. It's important to keep that connection with the other person, to let them know they're loved and desired.

You don't have to say "I love you" every five minutes, but a touch, a word, a note, whatever it is, it's important to maintain that connection so neither of you feels taken for granted—because that could happen.

❖

My husband and I have a couple we're friends with, and they've been married a long time like we have. They say it's very important every day to tell your partner, "I love you." My husband and I say "Love ya" all the time, and we mean it. But our friends tell us that the commitment, the love, should be pronounced every day as love, not "love ya."

129

It's got to be "I love you." That's really hard for my husband and me to say. It's so stuffy, and it has a different feeling. We laugh at each other because it's not natural for us.

❖

I think maybe it's an American thing to say "I love you" all the time. We're English, and my husband and I never say it to each other on the phone, for example, or in front of other people. We rarely even say it to each other in person. It's not that we don't feel it, but it's not the way we do things.

❖

I say "I love you" now more than I did early on. When I was younger and growing up in Asia, I took it as a negative that Americans say "I love you" all the time. I thought, "They don't mean it, and why would you say things you don't mean?" Now I've learned that you do it because you want to offer someone you love an assurance. Repeating it lets them know that.

Don't fool around with fooling around. Infidelity poses a threat.

Here's what I learned from the infidelities in my first marriage: first, I didn't realize I would ever be vulnerable to it. It honestly came as a surprise to me that I could cheat, so I know now to be vigilant about shutting down any potential for temptation. Second, what I did hurt not just me and my wife, but the whole community of family and friends surrounding us. And finally, what's the point? Having an affair doesn't fix anything. It just magnifies the negative things you already feel. Saying no to an infidelity will help your self-esteem ten times more than saying yes to it.

This may seem obvious, but cheating is no good for a marriage. It should be avoided at all costs. I once read that even the "moment of maybe" should be avoided. That moment you flirt or flirt back is dangerous. It's like unlocking a door. You may not have opened it, but you gave yourself that option. Keep that door locked up.

I know from experience that there are all kinds of rationalizations that can take place in someone's mind about why they might get away with a little fling outside the marriage. But at the end of the day, it's about love and respect. Infidelity is a selfish act. It's not usually done to hurt the other person, but it often does.

I've seen a lot of people cheat in their marriages. I've known the background behind it, and I'm protective of our marriage for that reason. I don't think my husband ever would have been open to communicating about that, except that I pushed for it right up front.

If you're with somebody who's a bit of a playboy and he's had affairs in the past, or he just has that attitude that it doesn't mean anything, well that's just a load of old rubbish. If it happened to my husband or me now, it would be a symptom of something seriously wrong with us; it wouldn't just be a little fling. I used to think it would be the end of us, but with children, I don't know if I think that anymore. It's hard to know, but it would change everything.

Faithfulness is very important for me and my husband, and we talk about it. My husband is Catholic by background, and that does kick in for him. I don't have any religious reference, but I wouldn't do it because it's wrong and hurtful, not for any other reason. We've always been very clear with each other on what we think about that.

It's very important to us that my wife and I have been faithful to one another for forty years, and we talk about it. My wife works with young, handsome men, and in my business, I have all kinds of temptations. Lots of my colleagues succumb to those temptations. I would tell anybody who wants to maintain a long-term marriage that it won't happen if you think you can have just the one affair—and I think people who have only one affair are a very small group of people anyway.

I'd say that people should be very, very careful about putting their marriages at risk by even a single indiscretion. Fidelity is very important in a marriage, and the human condition is such that we rely on the trust of our mate. The idea of somebody being unfaithful in the physical sense is an intrusion that can be extremely damaging.

I know that a lot of times, for guys, they're unhappy and the idea of an affair is just an idea. Pretty soon the idea becomes a flirt, and then the flirt becomes who knows what? I really talk to my husband about how important it is to be careful, because there are women out there who are looking for that. It happens the other way around, too, with men who hit on married women. Cheating doesn't just happen by accident. I think my husband could get tricked into that kind of thing if we got disconnected.

It's extremely important to both my husband and me that we're faithful to each other. It would devastate him if I had an affair. If he were unfaithful, I think I would recover, but not well. I used to think I would walk out the door, but I know these things happen, so I feel like if he did make a mistake I'd want to try to work it out. I think it would be very difficult, though.

At this point, and for the foreseeable future, we both feel that it wouldn't be infidelity that would break us up. We work hard on our romantic life, so it wouldn't be that we'd fall in love with some stranger because we were dissatisfied at home.

Romance in marriage means different things to different people. It may have little, or nothing, to do with sex.

The most treasured time I have with my wife is first thing in the morning. It's our most romantic time, and we cherish it more than any other time. We get up at 6:15 and sit down for an hour together, have a couple cups of coffee, and talk. We share what we think about things, talk about the day before, or what the day looks like today.

In the evenings, we both get home late from work, have dinner, watch TV, and then go to bed and fall asleep right away. There's nothing left, so that's why we both love the mornings. I get to work a little later than my colleagues, but so what? You'll always be behind; there's always stuff to do. That time in the morning belongs to my wife and me, and I won't trade it for anything. I refuse to give it up.

❖

When I was dating my husband, I used to get so excited before our dates that I needed to lie down on the floor to calm down. Romance now is a much more comfortable thing. I'm still excited to see him when he comes home at the end of the day, but there's no worry or anxiety.

I'm going to go out on a limb and say my husband and I have redefined romance. Stereotypically, people think of romance as that fluttery feeling, when you have candles lit around the house. We don't do that as often as we used to, and I don't long for it. The candles are still there if we want them. We can put the ambience in the air, but it doesn't feel like it's necessary. Our romance now is shared activities, like going on a hike or taking trapeze lessons together. We know we're going to wake up in the morning and have the entire day together. That's romantic. That's fun.

My husband and I met online, and sex was the reason we met. Now that we're married, sex is a lot more rare. We're more into the comfort of being together. We're very tender, giving each other flowers and candlelight dinners, snuggling and kissing and holding hands. To me, that's romantic.

The first few years with my husband were incredibly romantic. He wooed me, and I'm not going to lie, it definitely worked. Flash forward to now, and we don't do the traditional romantic stuff. That's mainly because of me, because I'm not a traditionally romantic person. I like cards, and I like flowers because I like acknowledgment of special dates. He does, too, but we don't go crazy about things like that. I think when you try to force romance into marriage, it *feels* forced. The romance for me comes in the small things that we do. We like to be together, and we don't actually like to be apart. We rarely do things without each other. We don't have a huge life outside of our relationship, and I think that's strengthened it.

I don't think romance applies that much to a relationship that's been around for a while. The notion of romance in my marriage feels a little false. We're not a romantic couple in the way we used to be, and I don't need it. The small and unexpected things are what make our relationship romantic. This morning, for example, I was cleaning the kitchen and listening to the radio. My husband's out of town at the moment for work. An old song, "Come Monday" by Jimmy Buffet, came on, and I teared up not so much because I was missing him, but because it reminded me of how much I love him. That's where the romance is for me.

When I look at my husband, it's not all lovey-dovey gushy. I just have intense feelings of admiration for his sweet nature, the way he parents our kids, and the way he treats me with respect, tolerance, and just kindness. He also can still really make me laugh. He does these musical revues for us at night, and I just love the way he is with our kids. What you think of typically as romantic and passionate isn't really there anymore, but the other stuff is just as powerful.

I'm not particularly romantic. My husband used to get me a single red rose every Valentine's Day, and then I got a little blasé about it. I think it was like, "Oh, there's another one of those." I think I've worn his romantic side down by being a little too practical. I've knocked it out of him, unfortunately, and I regret it, because I wish he'd do things like that now.

It's a myth that romance needs to be part of a marriage to make it last. I don't really feel like romance fits into my marriage. It only lasts for the first couple years, and then it's gone. It's like infatuation. Marriage is deeper than that. There's so much more that enriches your marriage besides romance.

Romance for my husband and me has a lot to do with stress levels. The romance ebbs and flows just like the feelings of strong love. We've been blessed in that we haven't had that many intense struggles as a couple. We do put a lot of pressure on ourselves career-wise, but we haven't had problems with in-laws, finances, or children. Sometimes when you're not feeling the strong affection, it's just because you're really stressed out. When we're on vacation, however, we're strongly in love with each other. We're together and go to dinner, and then we get to snuggle. Snuggling is pretty important to us. I don't think we spent a lot of time snuggling when we were dating.

I find that when my husband and I are in roles that are visually romantic, like a black-tie dinner, I become more romantic. Out in the backyard taking out the trash doesn't do it for me. I also still get turned on by the idea of being in a crazy environment, like going on a hike where there's nobody else on the trail. We just had our fortieth anniversary and went down to the Florida Keys, and we were walking through a canopy of trees. I kept saying, "Let's stay here, let's stay." I was feeling it at that moment.

I'm what you'd call a fairly romantic person, but that's not what really, in the long run, is wanted. My wife really feels loved when I do tasks around the house. She doesn't want the kind of romance that puts rose petals on the bed. She wants me to take out the trash and clean up the kitchen without being asked. She thinks it's romantic when I do that stuff because it makes her feel cared for. It makes her everyday life easier, and it shows her I'm in this with her.

136

The romantic moments are smaller, but they're still sweet. For example, we have these bantam chickens, and they were all supposed to be girls, but I think one of them is a boy. The other day I was telling my husband all about him, who's got furry feet and puffs himself up and takes on much bigger hens. And as I was telling my husband about it, he got this funny look on his face and gave me a big hug and said, "I love you." That was nice.

An incredible flip-flop has happened for my wife and me. When we started out, my wife was the starry-eyed bride who thought we were destined to be together, that it was the will of the cosmos. I was very utilitarian. I thought I chose her because she was the best person and the measuring stick by which I judged other women. She filled everything I wanted, and I chose her and made a decision to love her.

She found that very hard to take because, for her, our relationship was such an emotional thing, and it was destiny, and she found it impossible to believe that for me it was simply a logical decision. I tried to explain to her that there was the emotion, there was the passion, but sometimes, on bad days, I needed to tell myself logically that I made the right decision, because I didn't feel like I was in love with her.

But now it's really weird, because I've come to believe that we were destined to be together.

I think of romance as the pursuit. In dating, we had that pursuit, and that had a different feel. I now think of romance more as companionship. My wife and I spend more time enjoying each other. *Romance* is not the word I use. I feel more comfortable all the time but less excited. It's not as new or as startling; it's just something that I enjoy. Every way I try to describe it, it sounds not that great, but I'd definitely trade what we have now for what we had when we were dating.

Many long-married couples still have chemistry, and they work at keeping it alive.

My husband can be very romantic. One night we were out in the area where we went to school together as kids. He was driving all around and I said, "Where are we going?" And he pulled up in front of our school and said, "I thought we could make out."

My husband and I went through a major renovation to our home that took eight years. During that time, I grew to appreciate what I call "a swoon a day." You can get away with barely seeing each other, barely talking, and suffering through having the toilet in one room and the sink in another if you take a little time to connect every day. You need one affirmation every day, to take the time to let it soak in that your love is just as intense today as it was when you first met.

My husband and I have been through so many things. We've gone through things that have changed us and who we are, but as a couple, I've always felt we were still in love, as silly as it sounds. My friends tell me I still have goofy butterfly feelings, and there's still a glow for me when I see him.

My wife is as physically attractive to me as the day I married her. I'm surprised by that after twenty-two years. I don't know if that's a common feeling. Objectively, I figure she probably isn't as beautiful as the day I married her, but she does a good job of taking care of herself. I think it must be a grace of God that I still feel that way about her.

The attraction for us is still very present after eleven years of marriage. One of the things that drove my husband and me to know we needed to be married is that we had a long-distance relationship. It was physically exhausting, and we'd get sick immediately after parting. The attraction has always been very strong for us.

Sex isn't what marriage is all about, but it is part of the way you love each other. For my wife and me, our sex life has definitely gotten better over time.

Simple affection is one of the things we miss when my husband and I have to spend time apart. I sleep better when he's in the same bed.

Everything about sex is important. There's the release, and I don't mean physically. You're together, anything goes, and you're in the moment. Nothing else matters. You're not thinking about your daily responsibilities; you're not thinking about what you're waking up to tomorrow.

I still have an unmitigated attraction to my wife, and it's a really important element of our relationship. I don't think it's a cliché to say that relationships are work and marriages are work. The attraction is one of the main things that keeps us together. If that's not there, I think that's when couples start to fall apart.

Sex is still really, really important to us after more than a decade of marriage, and a sense of attraction to each other is very important. Sex is fun, it's light, it's nice, it's soft, it reconnects you. It shows the other person that they matter, that there's desire and attraction. It helps keep the flame. Otherwise you'd just be roommates.

Chapter 9

· ·

GOOD GIFT, BAD GIFT

The best way to remember your wife's birthday
is to forget it once.
—H.V. Prochnow

H AVE YOU EVER received a bad gift, something you really didn't want? If so, did something like the following interior monologue blast through your brain?

Oh, no. Oh, no, no, no. I can't believe you'd think this is something I'd want. Don't you know me **at all***? I don't know what to say. I really want to tell you I hate it, but you're looking at me with your eyebrows raised and grinning like you're in on a super special surprise...and you are! It* is *a surprise. Now what do I do?*

You remember what a simpler time it was before you unwrapped that present. You were a lot happier then.

This kind of thing happens to the best of us, and it's why gift-giving can be an ongoing source of anxiety. On at least four occasions a year—birthday, Valentine's Day, wedding anniversary, and Christmas or Hanukkah—spouses can strain to think of yet another perfect gift for their beloved.

That's a lot of pressure at regular intervals, and even long-married couples can scratch their heads when it comes to finding the right gift every time.

It sometimes seems like a no-win situation: If you don't know what to get, do you guess? If it's no good, do you get points for trying? Is it ever an acceptable option to do nothing?

Our happy couples have mostly sorted out the rules that work for them, but some confess that this is still a thorny area. Like everything else in a long, happy marriage, gift-giving is another category in which skills need to be learned, and mistakes will almost certainly be made.

Even happy couples
may have consistent trouble
giving gifts to each other.

My husband and I do not have a good history of giving gifts to each other. We've both given each other so many things we didn't like that now my husband is really insecure about the whole gift-buying thing. He's always asking people what I want. He has no clue anymore.

I've told my husband many times that I don't like orange flowers, and I don't like red roses. And how many times now have I gotten some orange tiger lilies or red roses from him? He says it's the peer pressure. On Valentine's Day he sees all these guys buying flowers and thinks he has to get something. You hate to look a gift horse in the mouth, but it has the opposite of the desired effect on me. Not only does he get the kind of flower I don't like, but he also goes to the grocery store to get them. He says he gets coffee and a donut at the same time and kills two birds, but come on. Yuck.

I am much less into giving gifts than my wife is. Years ago, I thought there were a couple of times when it seemed more convenient that we celebrate her birthday on the weekend before her actual birthday, so we did. Then on her birthday, well, she's funny. That is a special day. On her birthday, she needs to have a card and a gift. It needs to be *on* her day. Doing Valentine's Day on the 10th because it's cheaper? Nope. It doesn't even matter if I'm traveling; I've got to find a way to give her the gift on schedule. The times when I missed, she was in a funk all day.

Gifting is something I've had to learn about in our marriage. I think there's a huge thing that women, in particular, grow up with. We see gifts as a recognition of love. For guys, they need to gift well or pay the consequences. My husband's frugal nature certainly didn't make him a star at gift-giving early on, and I took it personally. I was definitely guilty in our early marriage of placing more value on that than I now think is right.

My wife and I decided this last Christmas that we weren't going to exchange gifts, and she always breaks the rule. When Christmas came, it was like, "Well, here's a book. And I got these socks for you." Meanwhile, I got her nothing. I thought we had an understanding. I took her at her word, and it wasn't like afterward she was really disappointed. I used to think I did a decent job of giving gifts to her, but I've lost it.

My wife's family is a family of IOUs. They don't do it with me, because I've made my feelings known, but they use them with each other. I think if you're going to give your spouse a gift, you have to work it out so you give them that gift on their day. It had better be an extreme exception, with highly mitigating, war-torn circumstances, that prevents that gift from being ready to go.

My husband once gave me something from Victoria's Secret. I think I was sixty years old at the time. He was usually good about gifts, but I guess this time he didn't know what to get for me. A friend told him to go to Victoria's Secret because they have nice things. The gift wasn't anything that risqué, but it certainly wasn't me. It was nice of him to try.

My wife and I have both given each other some bad gifts. She's given me clothing, and I haven't worn any of it. I think I've got MC Hammer pants from her in the back of my closet somewhere. We're learning, though.

The second gift I got my wife when we were dating, which I thought was one of the cutest, nicest things a boyfriend could ever do for a girl-friend, was to give her an engraved decorative state license plate with the name of her dog on it. She didn't appreciate it like I thought she would.

Over the years, my husband has given me wheelbarrows, pump sprayers, toasters, shovels, lawnmowers, saws, and cheese graters. I've never taken a present back. Even though it might have been a less ro-mantic gift than I yearned for, I think it's rude to reject a gift, no matter what it is. On the other hand, I buy him paintings, music, books, roses, and Godiva chocolates, and he pretends to love them, so we've figured out how to make it work.

My husband wasn't a gift-giver when we got married. During our first few years, he'd often forget special occasions, and I would cry and feel like he didn't care about me. He wouldn't forget the date or occasion, just that he needed to get a gift. He needed to be trained, and now he's a fabulous gift-giver. I forget it was ever like that, and he loves how happy gifts make me.

You tend to give what you want people to give to you, but you should think instead about what they'd like to receive. I learned about this from the book *The Five Love Languages* by Dr. Gary Chapman. He explains that each of us has a "love language," or a way in which we feel most loved. Partners often don't have the same love language, and then someone can feel hurt when there was no hurt intended. Some people are moved by gifts, others by acts of service, and so on.

I like gifts, and it doesn't have to be something big. It's the thought behind it. Like if my husband thought to stop on the way home and get a candy bar for me. Stopping to do that shows me he took time out of his day. I also like it if my husband washes the floor on a Saturday. That's a really good gift.

My husband and I are definitely of the mind that we give each other things when we know the other one wants something, rather than waiting for special dates and trying to top what you did last year. I definitely bought into gifting for all those occasions early on, and you just set yourself up for terrible disappointment. I realized this after years of him not giving me things that I thought maybe I should have. Then I realized that it was just fine, because when it mattered, he always came through. He's always done that, so if he failed at Anniversaries 101, then it really wasn't important.

Maybe you're trying to earn favor by giving a gift, but my wife and I have never related gifts to that. I don't think gifts have ever indicated to the other person, "This is how much I like you." I confess that sometimes I've felt like I had to go get my wife a gift, like at Christmas. Usually I wait until Christmas Eve, when they have everything marked down.

I can easily tell you the worst gift I ever got my wife. It was early in our relationship. She said she wanted to get in shape, so I got her some sessions with a personal trainer. Well, that was just like saying, "You're fat." She was very upset, and I think she may even have cried. I realized I'd really blown it, so we went out together and I ended up buying her a whole computer system. I spent like $5,000 because I felt so guilty. True story.

❖

I got some advice early on from some of my married friends who said never give appliances as gifts. If you need a new washer, go out and get it, but don't call it a gift. That's good advice.

❖

My wife really likes flowers, and I can never remember to get them for her. I hate to say this, but I have a reminder in my phone that goes off every so often that says, "Buy flowers." I usually look at it and think that I'll get them tomorrow. Actually, the irony is that I think today is one of those days. Yep, it's right here. Shoot.

Jewelry can be a dream come true. But just to be safe, make sure it's returnable.

For Christmas a couple years ago, my husband gave me a pair of earrings. They were so completely unlike anything I'd ever wear that I almost gasped when I opened the box. I thought of one of my aunts who has terrible taste, and I thought it looked like something she'd wear. I remember saying "thank you" and gushing about them a little. I appreciated that he went to the effort, so I kept them, but I don't think I've worn them even once.

❖

It was my wife's fortieth birthday, and she had dropped hints that she wanted diamond earrings. I guess I didn't think about it very carefully. You can't impulsively buy diamond earrings, and I wasn't going to spend a lot of money when I hadn't really thought it through. I knew the ones I got weren't that good, but I gave them to her anyway.

She said they were for a child—or even a baby. She was very disappointed, and I ended up returning them to the store. I had to live with that mistake for a while and think through how I was going to make amends. I did a lot of research and wrestled with myself about what to spend, because diamond earrings are expensive.

In the end I threw her a surprise party six months later, and I gave her several gifts, including the diamond earrings she wanted. She really liked the party, too. The effort is very important. It's obvious when you put the effort in and when you don't.

My husband and I had been together for a couple of years, and my sister talked him into buying me a piece of jewelry. The problem is that my sister and I have very different tastes. I call her "Mrs. Got-Rocks." She's way over-the-top for me, and jewelry is a really personal thing. So, I opened up this gift on Christmas, and he'd gotten me a necklace that was something I'd never wear. I had to tell him it was beautiful, because there were a lot of people in the room, and I thanked him.

Later, when we were alone, I told him I thought he should take it back. I told him for that kind of money, I'd like a new bathroom sink. That made him laugh, but after that he became reluctant to buy me anything. Now he usually asks me.

I always said the only watch I'd ever want to wear would be a really nice one, like a Rolex—nothing crazy, but better than average, something I'd get as a commemorative thing or a reward. My wife knew this very well. For my birthday one year she gave me this present, which was an awful watch that was about the last thing I'd ever want to wear. We have a good enough relationship that I said, "You know, I don't think I'm ever going to wear this. Why don't we return it and get a wallet?" So, that was okay.

The next year we went out to dinner again for my birthday, and she handed me this little gift box. I opened it, and it was the exact same watch she gave me the year before! She had clearly forgotten what happened the previous year and bought the exact same watch again, only with a different band. She tried to play it off by saying "I thought you just weren't ready for it last year," which made it worse. But it was really bad, really funny.

Last year we had our first baby, and my business was doing well. I'd cut a few pictures of watches from magazines, and unbeknownst to me, my wife acquired the watch of my dreams. Third time's the charm, and it only took five years.

When we were dating, my husband was working in Manhattan. He called me and said he'd gotten me a present. He couldn't keep it a secret, and he told me over the phone he'd gotten me a tennis bracelet with "colored diamonds." I didn't exactly know what that meant, and then when he gave it to me, it was like a charm bracelet you get from a cheap shop at the mall. He got it on a sidewalk stand—not exactly like shopping in the Diamond District in the city. We had a good laugh and I said, "thank you," and it was a sweet thought. I don't have it anymore.

Early on in our relationship, I noticed my husband didn't wear a watch. I asked him about it one time, and he said he'd lost his watch. So, I bought him a really beautiful, tasteful watch for Christmas. When he opened it up, he looked disappointed, but he didn't say anything.

He left it on the bedroom shelf for days until finally I asked him,

"Don't you like your watch?" Then he looked at me and said, "I don't wear a watch." Well, that would have been nice to know before I'd spent a thousand dollars.

Knowing the relationship that I have with my wife, I'd never go and pick out a diamond ring and spring it on her and say, "Here you go. I hope you love it!" That just wouldn't work. If we were going to buy a ring like that, it would be a deliberate thing where we'd pick it out together.

My husband and I used to joke early on about the fact that it was nice that both his mother and my mother left me some really nice jewelry, because it was very clear I wasn't going to get any from him. However, my brother-in-law gives my sister fabulous stuff from Tiffany, and their marriage sucks, so I've learned over the years that jewelry can be really overrated.

When it goes well, the perfect piece of jewelry can be the ultimate keepsake— and not just for the ladies.

The gift my wife liked the most is this set of diamond earrings I gave her. I was told—by her—that she could only wear diamond earrings. I assumed she was allergic or something, and she implied it but didn't say it. Of course, she was joking, but I didn't know. I don't mind because she wears them all the time. If you could ever wear something out, she'd have worn those out.

My favorite gifts have all been jewelry. My husband gave me jade bracelets when I gave birth to each of our boys. We were in Taiwan when we had our first child, and mothers there traditionally receive jade bracelets. When our second child was born, we'd moved back to the States. He had his mom, who lives in Taiwan, buy a bracelet from the jade market where he got the first one.

I feel like jewelry is a physical representation of love. It lasts more than a lifetime, and it's something I want to pass on to my children and grandchildren.

Gifts aren't important to me, but they were important when I wasn't receiving them from my first husband. When I started dating the man I'm with now, he gave me a gold watch. That was very important. It meant a lot because I had been neglected. The watch is a symbol that I was being respected as a woman for the first time at thirty-nine years old.

My wedding ring from my first marriage was bought cheap at a shopping mall, and it was literally in a set called "Ring-O-Love." It wasn't as special as it should have been. I'm not a jewelry-wearing kind of guy, but when my current wife gave me my inscribed, thick, platinum wedding band from Tiffany, I felt like, *This is the one piece of jewelry I can wear with pride*. I actually love it. It's symbolic on a lot of levels.

Don't make it harder than it needs to be. If your partner wants something, then just get it if you can.

Last year I kept a list during the whole year of everything my wife mentioned she liked, from artwork to books and a jacket, that kind of thing. I got her everything on the list for Christmas, and that was a big hit.

My husband always says he's bad at gift-giving, and usually he doesn't give me very much. But one year on my birthday I came home from work and he was sitting in the den with a giant stack of presents—not one present, but a big pile of them, all from Williams-Sonoma. He bought me an amazing knife and a lot of other stuff, including a mandolin. He'd heard me say I'd always wanted a mandolin but would never buy one for myself because they're so expensive. It was so thoughtful because we love to cook together. Each one of those gifts meant something.

One time I needed a new cell phone. When I left work and got in my car, my husband had picked one up, put it in my car and plugged it in. And it was pink. That was great.

❖

I wimped out the last few Christmases and gave my wife a certificate saying she can get anything she wants, for any amount, at any time she wants it during the year. Turns out, she loves that.

❖

For my fortieth birthday, my husband got me a Steinway grand piano. That went back to when we first bought our house and I remarked that the living room had a nice space for a grand piano. We had an old, used, upright piano. I never thought I would really own a grand piano; it was just something that came off the top of my head, but he remembered that I'd said it. It was about a year later when he got it for me. His secretary later told me that he left the office early so many times to shop for pianos, sometimes driving hundreds of miles away. I was so surprised. It was a wonderful gift.

It's not about you.
Think about what your partner wants,
not what you want for your partner.

Cards are something I've always found to be important. In fact, I've gotten upset with my husband for getting me a gift but not a card.

I always considered Valentine's Day to be a creation of Hallmark and a commercial holiday. Not participating is just my way of getting back at The Man, but when I didn't get my wife a Valentine's Day gift the first year, it was a major bust. She seems to think it's something more romantic than that. So, I've learned to participate and contribute to corporate greed, even though I don't strictly agree with it.

I never particularly liked camping, but my husband talked me into going one summer, and I could tell he was in his element. He just loved it. That Christmas I gave him a tent, but it wasn't just the tent he liked. It was putting my blessing on camping trips I'd take with him in the future.

My wife and I give each other three gifts for birthdays and Christmas: one's personal, one's practical, and one's sexy. The practical is usually something the other person has expressed an interest in. The personal is usually something very inexpensive that just has meaning, like I might give her a card that has a picture of cats on it because she likes cats, or a cat beanie baby. It's about recognizing a quality she has. Sexy gifts have been gift certificates for a weekend at a B&B, or lingerie or something. Her sexy gift to me has often been cologne, but the gift I have to give back, then, is a commitment from me to wear it. I can't believe she likes that stuff.

We were looking for a dog and decided to get this white one, but I'd gotten attached to a black dog we saw while we were looking. Unbeknownst to me, my husband talked to the woman who owned the black dog and had her keep him for three months. Then he came in one evening carrying the dog. Talk about your jaw dropping. To pay attention to that and to honor someone's heart's desire, that's a real act of kindness. We did have an odyssey training that dog, but he's great now. To me, that's the perfect example of a really awesome gift.

It's fun to melt someone's heart. Sentimental gifts can be worth the extra effort.

Nothing to me says "I love you" more than something handmade. I wanted to create something for my wife for our last anniversary. I found a little leather book that we bought in Rome six years ago on our honeymoon, and I filled it with drawings of all the different places we've gone together since we've known each other, where we met, where we've had vacations, romantic key moments in our relationship. She loved it. It's a keepsake.

On our birthdays every year, my wife and I exchange the same, twenty-five-year-old card. We always slip a little, updated note into the envelope, but we've passed that same card back and forth now for all these years.

On my fortieth birthday, my dad had just died. I'd been away with my family and came home, and two or three days later my husband said he had to run to the store for something. He actually went to the airport to pick up my sister, who he brought out for a week to surprise me. She was the person whose company I craved. It was just the nicest, nicest thing.

One of my favorite gifts from my wife: she collected all the love letters I gave to her when we were courting and put them together in a leather binder and gave it to me for our twentieth anniversary. She's good about gathering up things of significance and sentimental value and making sure we don't lose them.

My wife and I are love note people. Those notes will get hung onto forever. We have huge volumes and metal boxes of letters between us. I also think it's important to send notes through the mail. You can put them in envelopes and send them to each other at work. We'll also put notes in each other's suitcases if one of us is going on a trip. These things make more of a difference to us than gifts on special occasions.

❖

I had a certain coffee mug that goes back to the 1980s, a trigger-handle mug that was made by a potter and had the Smithsonian logo on it. It was a well-worn thing, and the finish had gotten all crackly, but I just loved it. It was the only mug I would use, and I broke it after using it for like fifteen years.

One day my wife was leaving for a trip with the kids and left a package on the counter with a ribbon on it. I opened it, and there was this Smithsonian mug, brand new, exactly the same as my old one. She knew how much I liked the original. It's not like she could run out to Target to get a replacement. It involved doing some research. That was very nice.

The first year we were together, I made my husband a CD of songs from when we were kids, because we went to eighth grade together. I went to the school, got a yearbook, copied our pictures, and put them on the cover. I put all the popular songs from that time on it, and he was so excited. He showed it to all his friends and thought it was the coolest thing ever. It was the best gift because he's a romantic and I'm not. That was part of the surprise.

One year my wife gave me a gift of a class in woodworking. I'd said I wanted to learn something about woodworking and get a little more proficient in doing stuff with wood. She bought me this class in which I made a gift box. It took months to finish staining and everything, and when I finished it, I gave it to her as a present. That made a nice, closed loop.

Last year for Christmas, I digitized all our old family home movies for my husband. It was really, really time consuming and pretty expensive. When he opened it Christmas morning, he actually cried. He doesn't really buy things for himself, and I really didn't know what to get him, so that was good. That was the best gift I ever gave him.

On my thirtieth birthday, my wife took me to an Irish pub, and I thought we were just having dinner. She gave me a box, and inside it were two tickets to Dublin. My family's mostly Irish, and as far as I know, I'm the first person in our family who's ever returned to Ireland. It didn't strike me at the time as a homecoming, but as we got ready to do it and we did it, it became more and more emotional to me. It was a great trip and was by far the best gift she's ever given me.

My birthday is in January, and I always had bad birthdays growing up. It's too close to Christmas, it was always cold and snowy so no one could come to a party, and my family wasn't very good about gifts. It all added up to significantly lowered expectations for my birthday.

A few years ago, my husband sold his 1965 Ford Thunderbird, which he'd had for many years, bought me a piano, and had a surprise party for me. I came home to all kinds of people at the house, a new piano, and no more car. It was amazing. I think I broke down and cried nonstop. I was psyched about the piano, but I'd never experienced the planning, forethought, effort, timing, friends, and surprise that he put together.

When I was growing up, my family was really iffy about gifts. My mom's idea of a birthday present would be to go to the Salvation Army, get a used baseball shirt that had someone else's name Magic-Markered in it, wrap it up, and give that as a gift. It was awful, so now I think that if you're going to give a gift, it doesn't matter if it's big or small. I don't care if it costs one cent or thousands of dollars. It should just be well thought out and real.

For some couples, gifts aren't a big part of life together—but they are appreciated when given.

For my fiftieth birthday, my husband got me fifty white roses. We don't usually give each other gifts, and it's the only time he's ever done that. That was really nice.

❖

My wife and I don't give each other many gifts, but we've never forgotten a date. Stereotypically, men are prone to forget that stuff, but in forty years, to my credit, I've never forgotten an anniversary or a birthday.

❖

In some relationships there's this big buildup about *What's he going to get me?* We try to be thoughtful and generous all through the year. Birthdays and Valentine's Day and Christmas are good opportunities to do a little more than usual, but there's not usually a huge burden of expectation on that day.

❖

My wife and I both appreciate an intelligent, thoughtful gift, and we almost appreciate the effort even more. This might sound silly, but the effort to wrap a gift, or hide it, or hand make a card is almost better.

❖

My husband and I think more together about the big picture. We spend more time thinking about what we need or want together. If we need to spend our money on a new deck outside, then I don't need a big diamond. Every now and then he brings me flowers for no reason. I'd rather have that.

Intangibles and shared experiences can sometimes make the best gifts.

The best gift my wife has given me is herself. All other gifts have very short durations.

To me, it's really sweet when someone writes something. In the old days, my husband would write me a long poem as a gift, and it would be really funny and clever. It would be an effort that he'd put into it every single year. For the last couple of years, I haven't seen one, but that always floated my boat.

My husband and I do a lot of joint gifts. We'll take a trip for a special occasion. When we travel, we like to come back with a memento we both like, like a painting from a street vendor selling watercolors, to remember the moment. We're expecting our first baby soon, and some people have asked me what he's going to get me when the baby arrives. He says he already got me the child, so I'm not expecting anything.

One year for our anniversary, my wife got a babysitter for the kids and surprised me. It was a Friday afternoon and she wouldn't tell me anything about it. We left in the early afternoon and went to a late lunch at our favorite place. I didn't know what else she had planned, and then she told me she had gotten us a hotel room in town. It was great.

At some point, my wife and I realized that we tend to buy the things we need. Now we view gifts as a way of getting together. We'll go for an experience, like taking a trip or going to a really nice restaurant and spending a small fortune. These are things we wouldn't normally do. They make nice memories, and at this stage, we're more interested in memories and events than we are in surprises.

It's uncharacteristic of me to spend a lot of money on anything, including gifts. When my wife was coming up on fifty, though, I decided we were going to have a trip, just the two of us. She wanted to do a horseback riding trip in Ireland, but I thought Africa sounded a lot more interesting, so we agreed to Africa. I didn't know how to ride, though, so I had to learn. We ended up expanding the trip, and we took our boys. It was spectacular, and it's become one of our defining elements. In our family, these have become known as Trips of a Lifetime, and it's the one thing I'm happy to blow ridiculous amounts of money on.

The best gifts I get from my husband are just his time and his willingness to do something he doesn't want to do at that moment. It could be something like going for a walk with me when he gets home from work and he's exhausted. To me, that's actually one of the best gifts he gives. I know he doesn't really want to do it, but he still does.

The best gift my husband has given to me is that he just lets me be, and he lets me be whatever I want to be. There's no set way I have to act. If I don't behave according to expectations, it's okay.

I think once you're satisfied in your life with your spouse and your relationship, you don't need a lot of gifts and adoration on holidays. If you're kind to each other on a day-to-day basis, that doesn't make it not special. That kindness is special in itself, and it's enough.

This sounds corny, but my husband says the best gift I've given him is making him realize there was real love again. We got together after he'd ended an awful, twenty-year marriage. In the first five years we were together, he really wasn't sure he believed in true love anymore. Now he says he didn't know what love was until he met me.

Chapter 10

FOR WORSE

If two stand shoulder to shoulder against the gods,
Happy together, the gods themselves are helpless
Against them while they stand so.
—Maxwell Anderson

M ARRIAGE PROVIDES NO GUARANTEE of living happily ever after. If anything, it opens people up to more heartbreak than they would have had if they'd stayed single.

The list of things that can go wrong in life is long. We can anticipate some of them, like a scary diagnosis or the death of a parent. Other disappointments can hit out of the blue. Someone loses a job. A hurricane strikes. A baby is born with health concerns.

We can't predict how we'll react to grief, sadness, depression, or disappointment until they hit. Whether the difficulties are foreseen or not, it's during these times that character is tested and marriages suffer.

There's no such thing as one person's pain in a marriage. The pain is always shared.

How can couples stay strong in the face of tragedy?

When one person feels broken, how can they find the strength to support their spouse?

And when do you ask for help from a professional?

One insight that emerged from talking to our happy couples is that time, talk, and compatibility, along with some of the other attributes discussed so far, can all work together to create a foundation with the strength to weather the storms of life.

Marriage won't shelter you from bad things. In fact, it may create difficulties you don't anticipate.

When you say "for better or worse," sometimes the "worse" is worse than you think it's going to be. I remember saying once, "I didn't know 'for worse' meant this."

It was an adjustment learning to be with my husband twenty-four hours a day, seven days a week. I wasn't prepared for it. I knew it in my mind, but I wasn't prepared for the actuality. Seeing my husband in his routine, with all the ups and downs, with the disagreements, it was a big adjustment.

It was a surprise to hit the bumps after we got married. I thought that you went to college, got married, had children, and lived happily ever after. I thought life would just get better and better. My parents' marriage was fantastic, and both my husband and I had lived sheltered lives. I was naive, but we didn't grow up with big problems and didn't know anyone who was divorced. After I had my second child, I had a lot of health complications, and we've had other challenges that we didn't anticipate. We didn't have any examples to follow, so we've had to learn on our own.

My wife and I had a child with special needs. I think something like 83 percent of couples who have special needs kids get divorced. There's financial, emotional, and societal stress. There's a sense of isolation and disappointment, and it was very hard on our marriage. What happens is that you have two people who are depressed living under the same roof every day, and that gets exacerbated by the situation. The relationship breaks apart not because you don't love that person anymore, but because you just can't take it. There's no animosity. You're just beaten down. You reach a threshold where you think, *This can't be the life I'm living*. Still, we've managed to stay together.

Our son has emotional problems and has made a lot of bad decisions with jobs and his relationships. He's made our lives very, very difficult at times. This has been a recurring problem, and it's brought a lot of stress to our marriage.

Before he came along, I remember thinking we had the perfect little family. After we had him, that evaporated. It changed our focus. It took over. To a large extent, we weren't nearly as happy as we had been before.

It wasn't until after my husband and I got married that I saw his tendency to be depressed. When it stuck around longer than an hour or a few hours and went into a whole day, I couldn't quite figure that out. I had never experienced that in my own family or in my self. He would mull over things, and it would feed his depression. Most of the time it would be short-lived, like he'd go to work and come home and be out of it. But in one particularly hard time in his professional life, he was involved in a lawsuit that went on for months, and it was very hard to deal with.

I decided that if my husband was down, I was sorry for him, but I couldn't get down in the pit with him. What good would that do? I had to learn to let him be and to try not to let it affect me. I tried to keep an even keel for the family and for myself.

Sometimes spouses are able to help each other in times of suffering. Other times, they are not.

I was diagnosed with cancer several years ago, and our marriage suffered during that time. When I think of those times, I don't think of much more than numbness and getting from one day to the next. It was a relentless thing, and it seemed like there was no room for anything but just getting through it. I think if we'd gone to support groups, they'd have helped. When one person goes through a sickness, the spouse often gets overlooked, and I think it probably was pretty bad for my husband. He didn't get the attention that I did. I got a lot of encouragement, and he was just left to soldier on.

Our daughter used drugs for a while, and we had a number of issues in dealing with her. One of the biggest problems this brought to our marriage was that my wife would side with our daughter, not with me. I'd see our daughter doing something harmful and tell my wife, and she wouldn't believe me. I got no encouragement or help and didn't have anyone to talk to. I felt abandoned, like I wasn't as important to my wife anymore.

Honestly, there were times during our marriage when I really thought I'd be better off alone. We had sick relatives and job stress and our own health stuff going on all at the same time. For a while there, it was touch and go. We had some very heavy-duty blowouts that were really tough and painful. There was tension between us, and a lot of sadness, pain, and fear.

There are people who have different thresholds for this kind of stuff, but my husband and I endured. If we'd been married to different people, maybe it wouldn't have worked. But we both understood digging deeper, getting our feet in the trenches, and deciding to fight to stay together.

❖

For me, I only knew one thing: fight, claw, and do whatever you have to do. I grew up in an Italian, Jewish, Irish neighborhood. They held me up against the fence and beat me until my father taught me how to fight. Then I gave an Irish kid a bloody nose, and he was my best friend.

My wife and I are both fighters. If either one of us came from a prima donna lifestyle or came from a life where everything was always right, we never would have survived all the bad things that have happened to us. In the neighborhood where we live now, most people are quite wealthy, and the divorces run rampant. They say there are more suicides among the wealthy than there are among the poor. People have breakdowns because they don't know how to endure. I always say you can lie down and play dead, or you can get up and fight. What do you want to do?

❖

My husband and I react differently to grief. When we've lost people we loved, I tend to go inward, and he goes outward and expresses anger. What I learned was that I had to choose how to react to his reaction. The way we all behave comes from our experiences. I let him be who he was and deal with it the way he needed to deal with it. And in that openness, we let each other be who we were, and that's how we came together.

If you just don't know what to do, that could be a sign that it's time to call an expert.

When you're really having trouble, don't try to do it yourself. It's like plumbing: my husband can't do plumbing. Every time he does it himself, it leaks all over the house. You gotta call somebody.

I didn't know I needed counseling in my first marriage until the roof was collapsing in on us. My ex-wife and I fought a lot and were growing further and further apart. What's sad is that I encouraged her to get counseling many times, but it never really occurred to me that I should get some, too. Eventually, I forced us to go to couples counseling, but by then, it was too late. There was so much damage that neither of us had the energy to rebuild.

I was not faithful in my first marriage, and neither was my wife. What's odd to say about this, now that we're no longer married, is that I believe our marriage could have survived. Ultimately, the affairs were a symptom of deeper problems. We both had issues in our past that we hadn't dealt with properly, and by that, I mean getting some good therapy and counseling. I think if we had dealt with those issues, the infidelities would never have happened.

A few years ago, we went through a hurricane that was pretty devastating. We were without electricity for two or three weeks, my husband's mother was living with us, and it was hot as hell. It was a really bad time. I can tell very quickly when I get depressed, and I watch out for it because I'm afraid of it. This time, however, everybody in the house was depressed.

I couldn't get my husband out of it. We'd had a few issues leading up to this, but I looked at him and said, "This is when we go talk to somebody." At first, he said no, and then I said, "This could be the one that does us in. If we don't get some help, we'll end up having some major problems and we could get divorced." Today he says, "I can't believe you threatened me with divorce," and I'm like, "It was not a threat, dude. I was not threatening." But if things hadn't changed, I would not have stayed in the relationship.

Sometimes in a marriage, one of the parties will need to look at the bigger interest of the whole relationship. I had enough experience to look out for the whole relationship, because he couldn't see clearly at the time. I think that's something that happens to couples. If they're not necessarily having a great marriage, where one of them gets a little distressed or is in quicksand, you have two choices. One is to say you won't put up with it, and it gives you an easy out. The other is to realize that you really want it to work, acknowledge that your spouse isn't doing very well, and step up to see what you can do to get it back on track.

Sometimes you reach the end of your rope with your spouse. When you do that, are you going to say it's not worth it? Since we've had the same arguments over and over and we can't find a solution, should we just quit? That's when you need to see if there's someone else who can help make it work. My husband and I had a time where we needed to talk to someone and see if we could go down a different path. I've seen relationships that broke up, and to me the biggest mistake those couples made is that they didn't go to therapy. They needed someone to help them. One of the best decisions we've made in our marriage was the decision to get outside help.

Professional advice is especially helpful in providing tools to deal with conflict.

When we got help, our marriage wasn't in trouble, but we wanted a third-party opinion about some of the things we'd been disagreeing about. It was a learning experience. It was like going to school or taking a class in better marriage.

When my wife and I went to see a therapist, he told us that we were having issues not because of what we said but how we said it. Presentation is everything. You can say, "You're a real jerk," or you can say, "I think you made some mistakes today. Let's sit down and discuss it." He really helped us look at the words we were choosing.

My husband and I both have tempers. We're not mild-mannered people, and we don't shy away from conflict. But over the last eleven years of being married, we've had to learn to deal with conflict in a way that's a lot less volatile. It started after we got engaged and started living together. We fought a lot and decided to get some counseling. We needed to fix how we fight, how we argue, and understand what we're arguing about, and it helped.

My wife and I had been married for nine years when we decided to go into counseling. We were concerned our marriage wouldn't survive. At that time, we were in our late thirties and still growing. It took care of some conflict resolution issues, which was good, but it also allowed us to take a step back and reassess our own values, and then to look how our values were interfacing. We all go through life doing our thing. Sometimes it helps to take a step back and see how you're doing on the continuum.

I've always been a lazy communicator, verbally, my whole life. There's a lack of precision in the way I communicate. When my husband and I saw a therapist, she identified the way I communicate, but at the same time, she said that my husband needed to be more patient with me.

The sum of our challenges over the years mostly comes down to my not communicating clearly enough, or his not being patient enough, or a combination of both. I can't think of an example where that hasn't been behind it.

Nine years into our marriage, my husband and I had counseling. We had a two-year-old and a six-year-old who needed me all the time. I was feeling put upon, and I was trying to balance a job at the same time. My self-esteem was low, I was needy, and I was looking outside for people to recognize me. I didn't know if our marriage would survive. We went to therapy together, and we still have the book our therapist had us read. More than thirty years later, some of the things he told us still come back. Whenever I'm having a difficult time, I reflect on that.

I think my husband and I actually need some professional counseling right now. He spends a lot of time away from home for his job, and every time he comes home we have to get reacquainted again. He'll be gone for a month or maybe more, and I get into a certain way of doing things. Then when he comes home, we have to start from scratch. We're not relating well to each other at the moment. I think we can fix this, but we need different tools.

My wife and I took a marriage course and learned the idea of "checking it out." Don't assume that whatever happened was intended to be hurtful toward you, even if you got your feelings hurt. Assume the person who married you actually loves you and didn't mean to hurt your feelings.

I went through a difficult time with my father at the end of his life, and I took it out on my family. My husband and I weren't connecting, and I thought that he hated me for it. We've never been to a marriage counselor, and we've never even really talked about going to one. We have a negative, knee-jerk feeling about therapists. I don't know why, but both of us feel this way.

I think now, though, that having an objective voice when you get into a negative pattern might have been helpful, rather than struggling through it the way we did. I definitely think it would have been at least a conversation starter. We eventually got unstuck, and I don't even really know how. I do know that we probably said more hurtful things to each other than we needed or even wanted to during that time.

My husband and I have had rough patches over the years, and we went to counseling once. He was having a forty-year-old midlife crisis, and we were clashing on everything and weren't connected. My step-father had just sold our family home and had to move in with us for a while. Our children were young and pretty needy, and our sex life had gone downhill as well.

I was a little frightened because I wasn't sure how my husband felt at the time, so we went to a counselor for about six weeks, one night a week. It was helpful. Years later, we still remember bits and pieces of things we learned. I think it's good to get an outside perspective. It helps to be able to talk in the presence of someone else who's sort of a referee, who bounces ideas back and forth. It's nothing to be ashamed of, and I'd definitely go again. If you value your marriage, it's worth doing.

Couples therapy isn't the only option. Sometimes one partner needs individual help.

When I met my husband, my sexual orientation was a big secret I'd been carrying for fifteen years, ever since I was sexually aware. I was always secretive and had a lot of things I couldn't talk about, and it all made me very depressed. When I had relationships before, usually they'd last six months or less. I'd just get a new one when things got hard. But when I met my husband and started to get serious with him, my depression got worse because I cared about him. It's like the relationship forced me to make some big decisions I wasn't ready for.

It was his suggestion that I get some help; he was also doing individual therapy. I think he even helped pay for it. Our relationship couldn't go forward until we dealt with our individual issues. After I came out, I had better, more open relationships with my family and close friends. The burden was lifted from my shoulders. I have nothing to hide anymore.

A few years back, my wife was going through some stuff. She was unsure about everything. She said she'd had enough, and that if this is what the marriage was, and what life was all about, then she didn't want it. There was nothing bad going on. Our kids were great, we had good jobs and a great life, but I couldn't help her. She went to a counselor, and it definitely helped.

After my first marriage ended, I went to individual therapy. The therapist helped me find my way out of depths and back into life. She asked me why I was there and what I wanted to accomplish, and I said, "I feel dead, and I want to feel alive." Counseling helped me realize that I'd shut down. I believe that the secret to life is passion, and it's probably the secret to marriage, too. I'm not talking about sex. I'm talking about enthusiasm.

I always give people the same advice about considering counseling, based on my experience. Both people in the couple should sit down with a piece of paper and write out the top five things they think are on each other's mind. Then you compare and see how well you do and whether you're in tune with the other person. If you're not fairly well matched up, you'd probably benefit from seeing a counselor. That's what my wife and I did, and it's made it easier for us since then, a lot easier. If you go to counseling, go with the goal of better understanding what's going on with your partner.

I went through a period where I was very unhappy personally. I was out with my husband, and we'd just taken this incredible motorcycle ride, and yet I was completely unmoved. I didn't care. I wasn't enjoying it at all, and my husband said, "What's wrong with you?" I had to confess, "I really don't know." Then he said, "All I can tell you is that I don't care how long it takes. Take as much time as it takes to figure it out, and do whatever you have to do. I'll be waiting for you when you come back." So, I went to counseling, and it really helped.

When I was married the first time, I was faking my way through life. I was disconnected on the inside and didn't know how to be alive with anyone, especially my ex-wife. Therapy gave me a way to crawl around in the basement to find the fuse box, replace the shorted-out parts, and then get some lights on, maybe for the first time. Of course, once the lights are on, you see the mess you've been living in and that you have some cleaning up to do.

If I could go back in time to my younger self, I would implore that the sooner you can figure out how to empathize with other people, the

174

more successful you will be in your relationships, your work, your life, and especially your marriage. It's a core value and something my wife and I both try to practice. You have to put yourself in your partner's position. When you think about how someone else is living and experiencing their world, it does change the way you communicate and interact with them. We actually learned this in therapy. You've got to stop being self-centered enough to put yourself in your partner's position sometimes. Empathy is the route to a more fulfilling relationship.

A few years ago, my husband and I went through a terrible time when my mother was diagnosed with cancer. She had an acute episode, and I went to be with her. My husband couldn't go with me, so we were separated for a while.

When I got back home, I was extremely depressed. I wanted to get cancer, too, so I could die with my mom. I wasn't suicidal or anything, but I was severely depressed and had no energy for my husband. He couldn't help me, and it took a while for me to realize that I needed the help of some of my old girlfriends. There was a lot of stuff that happened in my family, and I needed people around me who knew my history. Men also don't have the same relationship with their mothers that women do. I expected my husband to give me the same kind of support I could get from my girlfriends, and he couldn't. It was also important that these girlfriends were really supportive of our marriage.

My husband was really understanding and wasn't offended that he couldn't give me what I needed. He gave me space and encouraged me to talk to my friends. That was a really bad time in our marriage, but the lesson was a good one. I learned it the hard way, and I wish someone had told me I might need support from someone other than my husband.

Hard times can refocus partners on their goals for life and marriage.

In the long run, going through difficult periods matures you in a way. The experiences we've had with my wife's cancer and the deaths of our parents have had a profound effect on both of us. It's helped me keep things in our marriage in a more appropriate and productive context, I think. I focus now on what I think is important.

I know people who have left their relationships when it got hard. When my husband lost his hearing, someone I knew asked if we were going to stay together. I said, "What kind of question is that?" I guess there are people who might not stay, but I'm not that person, and that's not our relationship.

My wife says the things that have happened to us have changed us over the years, but I don't think they have. We have grown, and we don't see each other as seventeen-year-olds anymore but as middle-aged people, but we are still who we are. We've had terrible things that have happened to us, but we've always been on the same page about attacking them together. That's made us stronger.

My husband and I have been through so many things in our marriage that have tested us, but I would say that, overall, if you look at the essence of the person you're married to, all the other stuff goes away. I see a husband who has all the values and character attributes that are important to me. Because we've been through such big stuff, the day-to-day annoyances don't matter to me as much.

My husband and I have both gone through some very low points with my cancer and deaths in our family. I now feel like I have a limited amount of emotion to invest, and I'm not going to go looking for things that annoy me. After you go through the really hard, trying things of life, the more important things stand out. We don't wallow in our own hurt feelings or think about what might be unfair in life. I think that's one of the byproducts of going through difficult times. Maybe people who have had a carefree background can indulge in more of that self-pity, but we try to preserve what's good and nurture the good.

I got pregnant when I was twenty-four, and my husband and I were five years into our marriage. We went through natural childbirth classes and everything together, and it was going to be the first grandchild and a big event for our family. Then we lost the baby at seven and a half months. We were driving back from a vacation, and we had to stop at a hospital because I started delivering. It was a little girl, and she was stillborn. They asked me to name the baby and everything. Then when we got home, the crib had been delivered, we had to tell everyone what happened, and it was just all bad stuff.

That was the first traumatic experience my husband and I had together. I think it helped that one of us wasn't more depressed than the other; he was hurt as much as I was hurt. We've also been pretty religious our whole lives, and we believe certain things happen for a reason. I had a year of college left to finish, and after we lost our baby, I took that time to get my degree. When I graduated, I was pregnant with our son. There are a lot of statistics out there about how traumatic things break people up, but I think what helped us is that we both were convinced that what happened, happened for a reason.

I wouldn't want to go through all the tough stuff we've had in our lives again, but I think it's helped our marriage get better over the years. People really need to find the positive aspects of every mountain they climb and every obstacle they face, because there are lessons to be learned in everything. There are growth experiences in everything. Our marriage got better after each difficult event. We were stripped of everything, and in that process, we became more of who we wanted to be.

After our daughter died, I don't think I existed for an entire year. But we also had a new baby who was five weeks old. And life is interesting, because you think about what people survive—the Holocaust, genocide. It's amazing what people can survive. There's always life. There's always laughter and there's always joy. You never forget, but you move on.

I want my husband to be happy, and he wants me to be happy, because we've been through such hard times. We want to have a good time, we want to laugh, we want to have fun together, we want to be with our kids. We want to be together. We want it so much more because we've seen the other side.

Though it's not guaranteed, a strong marriage really can ease the pain.

My husband and I just had our first baby, and it's a big adjustment. There are all these things we used to do together that we can't do anymore, because our focus is on our daughter. I haven't been able to put nearly as much into my relationship with my husband as I used to. I work with other working moms, and we're all unrealistic about what we're capable of doing. We're completely split in half.

Recently I was feeling really pulled apart from my husband. I'd just gone back to work, and I felt like I was losing him, and I was crying and very emotional. And he said, "This is just now. This isn't forever." And that was an important thing for me to hear. It was exactly what I needed at the time.

We had some really rough financial difficulties a few years ago where we were stressed out beyond belief. I went to bed at night being so thankful that my wife was there to help me get through it. She was taking care of all the pieces of our life that I couldn't focus on because I was working so hard to keep us upright.

At one point my husband was forced to leave his job, and we were really broke. We didn't know where the next paycheck was coming from or whether we were going to be able to afford gas for the car, and it was really scary for a while. Ultimately, I think it did make us stronger as a couple and refocused us on what's important. We learned not to get too worried about the things we can't control. I was pregnant at the time, and our marriage gave us a different perspective. Jobs and money aren't everything. We stepped back and looked at the big picture and everything we already had, and that helped.

Our marriage helped my husband because my family enlarged his support net. First his mother died, then his father got brain cancer, so within just a couple of years, he didn't have parents anymore. My dad was a doctor, and he helped my husband understand what was happening with his father's illness. These were in-laws: they weren't my husband's real family, but they were closer than a lot of people were during that time.

❖

The first day my husband invited me out is the day I found the first lump in my breast. We weren't even dating then. I had surgery, then a second surgery, and by the time we started dating, I was having radiation every day. Our relationship started in parallel with my cancer, and it's been totally linked to the cancer.

When he met me, I was a single mother with a daughter, and I was active, working, and traveling. I told him, "If you take me, you take everything." By that, I meant my daughter, my background, and my world, which is pretty complex. He took it all, but he had no idea, and neither did I, what he was getting.

My treatments meant I had to stop working, and suddenly I was home full-time. I was on a raw food diet for a year and half, and he did it with me. At one point I was told I had three to six months to live, and he gave me an engagement ring in front of all our friends. For the past five years, he's been working for the two of us. He took everything over.

He refuses to accept that I owe him my life, but I do. If I'd had to work and do everything, I wouldn't be here. And I definitely would not be in the remission I'm in now. It's the first relief we've had. I'm still on chemo, and I will be until I don't know when, but I'm doing well. I have hardly any side effects, and my chemistry is perfect. We don't know what will happen, but right now, I'm the healthiest of people—and I owe it all to him.

Chapter 11

....

THE POWER OF TWO

The goal in marriage is not to think alike
but to think together.
—Robert C. Dodds

CRAZY BUT TRUE: marriage makes people stronger. I know I prom-
ised that there wouldn't be science in this book, but I need to
break the rule for just one moment here for a peculiar little study.

According to research done at University College London in 2019,
married people are stronger than widowed or single people. For one
thing, the study says that married people walk faster.

Who among us hasn't thought to themselves, *Gee, I'd love to walk
faster*? Just get married, and evidently you get that for free.

Another benefit, according to the study, is increased grip strength.
Married people have stronger handshakes and the ability to open pick-
le jars without help.

Now, as if those two perks aren't enough, our unscientific, happy
couples report that there are even more benefits to being married. Becoming a team seems to have a lot of advantages.

How do couples make themselves stronger over the years?

And what are some of the other rewards of being married?

The couples say that their marriages have given some of them a perspective and purpose they never had as singles, a richness to life they never knew possible. As the years pass, they continue to invest themselves with abandon and an iron grip.

In happy marriages, spouses treasure their partner's complementary skills and attributes.

One of the reasons I married my wife is because she has such good teeth and I don't. I thought that at least our kids would have a chance.

I'm a finisher and my wife's a starter. This has worked out fairly well in our marriage. She starts about twice as many things as she can finish, and I wind up picking up the pieces. One time she got this idea that we should start keeping bees. I told her that sounded fine. I arranged to go pick up some bee supplies and some bees and brought them back and set up a beehive in our backyard. Then she said, "Oh, you're keeping bees," and from then on it was my beehive. That's just one example of many.

My husband is an optimist by nature, and I'm not. I look to him so often for comfort when I'm worried about something. Just a few words from him about something I'm super worried or uptight about, and then it's over for me. I don't need to worry about it simply because he doesn't worry about it. It's very calming for me when he weighs in. Worry is a waste of time, we all know that, but it's a function of growing older. You get experience and age and start to know the things that can happen and go wrong. I'm more and more the pessimist than I used to be. I hate to think it's my trademark now, but my husband really helps me back away from that.

❖

One of the reasons I wanted to marry my wife was that her personality and values were a good blend of all the things I needed. I know now for the rest of my life and our children's lives, they'll have discipline, focus, direction, emphasis on education, and all these things I didn't have growing up. I didn't grow up in a big family, and she did. All those things were going through my mind even when we were dating, and they're extremely important to me.

It's interesting looking over our marriage so far. My wife and I have taken turns in certain roles and in being the primary breadwinner. It's never been a competition. We've both been so grateful to each other and completely supportive of each other in whatever role we happen to be in at the time.

I'm a lot more fragile than I appear to most people, and my husband knows that better than anybody. He knows I need him. He's there and likes to remind me that he's there. For him, I play the cheerleader role. He can get depressed or a little withdrawn, and it's my job to keep reminding him how great we have it and how great he is.

My husband and I have a fourteen-year age difference, and I was in my late twenties when we met. For the first ten years, his patience was the anchor of our relationship. Thinking back, I expected him to be more responsible because he was older. The fact that he was patient with me gave me self-assurance. It told me that he really loved me and wanted this lifetime relationship to work. Now I try to be patient: I learned that from him.

Marriage can be a superpower, helping people achieve individual goals they otherwise wouldn't.

I've traveled a lot more as a result of meeting my wife, and I've done more in general. I feel like I get more life and enjoyment because of my marriage.

❖

My husband says he wouldn't have graduated from college without my influence. When we met as students, he liked to party and have a good time. I was the studious one. After we got together, we still partied, but I had the discipline to say when it was time to study.

❖

My wife is a wonderful person to be around, morally correct, and she knows how to deal with people. I have, without question, become a better person with her influence than I ever would have been without.

❖

I ran a marathon last year. It's been on my checklist to do in life, and I've liked running since high school, but I never ran long distance like that. I have a friend who's a runner, and I wanted to lose some baby weight. She put the idea in my head that we could do it, but my husband is really the one who helped me achieve it. It was such a long training period. So many times I thought, *This is it, I can't do it, I'm not going to be able to finish, I don't have time,* but he was willing to help and watch the kids when I needed to run for four hours straight. I don't think I could have done it without his help emotionally, physically, or logistically. So, I did it. But I won't do it again.

❖

I'm very athletic now, but I didn't grow up that way. When I met my husband, he was really into Ultimate Frisbee, and I thought I might as well play because I liked him. Now we're training for a triathlon, which was my idea. I look at my family and the way I grew up, and I can't imagine living that way now. It seems so dull. I wouldn't have tried half the activities we've done on my own—and it's all because my husband encouraged me and told me I was good at things, even when I probably wasn't.

Earlier in my life, I didn't have big career aspirations. My career wasn't that important to me. When I met my wife, though, she's always been so successful and focused from an early age, and that really rubbed off on me. It gave me aspirations and dreams as far as money and promotions and trying to reach for the stars. My family always believed in me, but they were like, "We'll accept you as you are." My wife's attitude was, "I love you for how you are, but I love you enough to believe you can achieve even more in your life." She taught me that how hard I work will determine the success I have. She's one of my role models.

My wife had to take a graduate course this past year, and it was awful. We had to sacrifice time together and with our daughter because she had to be in school two hours a night, three times a week. I'd take care of our daughter so she could get her work done. We sucked it up and sacrificed, and we got through it by working together.

I'm not an overly ambitious person, though I'm not an underachiever. I went to college, and I was a fun guy. Academics weren't important to me: having a good time was more important. But when I met my wife, I started becoming more serious, because I wanted her in my life.

I went to law school and got into it and liked it, but I can reach a certain comfort level where I'm happy with my life as it is. She encouraged me to take another step, to take opportunities that were presented to me. I didn't dream of being a judge like I am now. I had abilities I never gave myself credit for. I give her credit for the motivation and making me realize some of the talents I didn't realize I had.

Women make men human, and without them, men would just be dogs. When I met my wife, I was floundering in life. I didn't have a sense of community, family, or career. I was having fun, but I was lacking meaning in my life. What she gave to me was a wholesomeness, a sense of well-being, a community in family. Since then, it's just grown. She feels that I've done a lot for her, but what she doesn't see is what she's done for me. What she's done for me is a thousand times more than what I've done for her.

My wife is a constant source of encouragement and affirmation for me, and she makes me believe I can do things that I probably wouldn't attempt otherwise. She's good about saying, "I'm proud of you. You do this amazing work. That was incredible." She's effusive in her praise, which makes me feel appreciated and capable and sometimes willing to take on more.

❖

I bought a couple of stores a while back, and I couldn't have done that without my husband's support. It wasn't the kind of thing somebody could do by themselves. He was that true partner who would do anything I needed him to do at any time. He wasn't on the payroll for most of the time, but he never resented the long days, the 24/7 kind of work that it was, the late-night emergencies and all kinds of stuff that came up over the years. He was extremely supportive in that endeavor of mine. I couldn't have been as successful as I was without him.

❖

The goal is to become your best self with someone, not your worst self. That's something I think about a lot. I have fallen into the trap once or twice of thinking, *Well, if I didn't live here with my husband, then I could do this and that, and darn it, here I am.* But that comes and goes very quickly. My husband gives me a lot of encouragement and support, and he's actually been a big factor in what I've been able to accomplish.

This makes me want to cry, but it's true: almost everything I have in my life now is because of my husband. All through my years of growing up, I struggled with insecurities, whether it was boys, friends, or school, thinking, *Am I smart enough? Am I pretty enough? Am I skinny enough?* I never thought I was smart enough to accomplish anything. There was another part of me buried underneath that said, "You are smart enough, and you are going to make it," but I had no idea how.

I went to school and had been working on myself when I met my husband. And with him, somehow all the crap fell away and the person underneath could shine through. He pulled it out of me. He saw the things I'd done in my past as life accomplishments, whereas I just saw them as part of my screwed-up journey to figure out who I was. He encouraged me constantly and believed in what I wanted to do in my work and life. It felt like there was no limit for him in what he saw in me and what he thought I could accomplish, and he's still like that.

Before I got married, I definitely had a period of time where I thought, *What am I getting myself into?* My husband is very different from me. I made a conscious choice to marry someone who would push me and challenge me and not let me just do my thing the way I wanted to do it. I spent most of my life being bossy, getting people to do the things I wanted them to do, and I dated a bunch of guys who worshiped me. I didn't want that in my life.

Neither one of us is interested in being complacent. I knew when I married him that he was the kind of person who'd always ask the hard questions. I love and honor that aspect of him. If you're honest about what you want from your partnership and the kinds of things you want in your life, and you have a strong chemical attraction to your partner, then you've got it made.

A team approach to life can increase a couple's ability to achieve ambitious goals.

My husband and I are certainly better because we've had each other, especially when our kids were little. There were times when we literally looked at each other and said, "I've got your back. Let's go." I also think that you can take more job stress if you have someone else to come home to.

If I hadn't met my husband, I would still be in the same apartment I lived in twenty years ago. My plan was to live there, pay it off, and have a downtown apartment with no mortgage. When we got married, he said, "This is yours. I want to make a home together." Boy, that was a big deal, because I was going to live there until I died. But it was reasonable for him to ask that, so we sold all the furniture and made a home together. It changed our trajectory for me to follow his advice. We upgraded, and we now have two homes, one of which we rent out. Having a team approach has changed my life a lot, and financially we're in a much better place.

My wife and I bought our house for a ridiculously small amount of money ten years ago. That year no house on the street sold for less than this one. It was a total piece of crap, a true tear-down. We were scared, but we didn't know what we didn't know. We should have probably known something by the fact that it didn't have any appliances, had a large hole in the roof, and the circuit breakers were literally rusting because water would flow into them—all of which was identified in the inspection, and all of which we ignored.

However, we took it upon ourselves to renovate, and it became us against the house for the next eight years. I have hundreds of books and several key mentors. I taught myself carpentry, plumbing, and electrical, and rebuilt this house, replumbed it myself, rewired it myself, and I feel very confident about the inspections. My wife was always the gravy train, cooking food for me and my friends and day laborers who worked with me. We got to be very creative in thinking about colors, wood, design, light, and architecture. It brought out the artist in both of us, and we've made it a beautiful space. We never could have done it without one another's support.

My wife and I met through work. She was a client, and I was the person trying to please the client. I sometimes joke that the relationship hasn't changed at all since then. We've struggled since we've been married with the idea of working together. I believe we have complementary talents and experiences, but we've worried about differences of opinion, conflict, and who'd take the lead on certain decisions. We've been dancing closer and closer to this idea for years, and now we're finally starting a business together. We haven't figured it all out yet, but we're ready to try it. I think we'll make a great team. Just like with our lives, we have so much more potential by being together.

I always wanted a spouse who'd be my partner. When I was a teenager, someone asked me how I'd define marriage, and I said it was the institution by which two people face the trials of the world as one. I still believe that to be true. I want someone who sees all the various struggles we go through as something not faced by him or by her, but by us. Even if only one of us is actually dealing with it, it's a struggle that both of us will confront.

Two against the world. Some happy couples become stronger by moving away from their families.

Moving around was the best thing that happened to us in our marriage. If we'd stayed where we were, we would have been very mindful of comments from both sides of the family, and we would have had a lot of parental input. It was good to get into a whole new situation where we had to face new challenges together, because the differences and baggage we each brought into the marriage disappeared.

An important part of our life was all the moving that we did. We moved every two years. We had each other, we had to find new friends, and that was it. We moved because we had to, and it was really good for us.

My husband took me away from my family when he went off to graduate school, and that was good for our marriage. It was nice to be able to see other places in the world and meet other people, and it was good for us to learn to make it on our own and not depend on family. I think you need to learn to be independent and rely on each other, and not go home to your parents or siblings and say, "Boo hoo, this is what's happening." You have to learn to grow, to live on your own.

Happy couples may lean on each other increasingly over time—even though it will eventually make parting more difficult.

My wife was away for work this week, and life just wasn't as enjoyable. When she's not here, things seem really disjointed. Then she gets back and starts yelling at me and I think, *What was I missing?* I'm kidding, but even though it's not all rosy, life just isn't as good without her.

One time I had this horrible, miserable day. I'd gone to the grocery store, and because of the way our condo is, it's a big deal to carry stuff upstairs to our home. I had all these groceries in the car, and it was 9 at night, and I was completely exhausted.

I called upstairs to my husband and said, "I'm just pulling up in front of the building. Would you mind terribly helping me carry this stuff upstairs?" He said, "Oh, sweetie, I'll be right down." He hung up the phone, and I literally sat in my car and cried. It was so sweet. He didn't grumble. He just hung up the phone, and there he was. He's so giving in a million different ways, and the simplest kindness can get to me. It was an action that said we're in it together. It made me feel like we were a unit, and I'd never had that in a relationship before.

My wife and I have a ten-year age gap, so when I'm sixty, she'll be fifty. Health-wise, how am I going to feel about doing things she still wants to do? On one hand she may keep me young, but on the other hand, am I going to slow her down? Those things weigh on me. Maybe it's how you approach it. If you want it to age you, it'll age you. If you want to act old, you'll be old. I think the onus is on me to stay young— or for her to be more understanding, one of the two. If she thinks I don't listen now, wait until then. I'll just turn off my hearing aid.

I consider myself independent, but I'm extremely dependent on my husband. He's dependent on me, too, and I think that's good, but we're not needy. We'll do things on our own, and we don't seek out advice from each other on every little thing. Dependency grows out of being married for twenty-five years. We know each other's strengths and weaknesses, and we fill in for each other.

I was thirty-six when we got married, and I didn't expect that so late in life. I felt like I lost my identity for a while, but the positive that came out of it was that I shed a lot of old bad habits and got to the core of who I was. My husband is a mirror reflection of me. You look at your partner, and, if it's a good relationship, they reflect back the good stuff about you. They nurture that and encourage that. Once I let certain parts of myself go, there was more room to become that whole person I wanted to be.

❖

Part of me dreams about the future, and I see my husband and me having enough money to be able to run our own business together—something that's not our lifeline but that we could do together. We both love our work and we love talking about our work. I don't see myself going out to play bridge with the ladies while he goes to golf. We would die immediately in that kind of retirement scenario.

At the same time, I try not to dream too much about retirement because, truthfully, I worry that I'll lose him early. We've had people close to us that we lost in their fifties. My husband has a stressful job, and he eats a lot of crap. In our case, I'm kind of in limbo. Part of my brain thinks about our future together, but there's a part of my brain that doesn't want to.

One thing my husband and I have talked about in the last year or two is mortality, and we haven't really talked about it before in thirty years. Both of us have had some physical problems we've been blissfully without in the past, and we've seen my husband's father's issues as he ages.

If you look at the actuarial tables, it's likely my husband will die before me, and that scares me. I don't think I'd be very good on my own. He's always encouraged me to find another life partner if that happens. I know he means it, but they don't grow guys like him on trees.

There are different seasons to life. Our kids are getting older now, and it's a different time than when we never got out the door by ourselves. In the next season, we'll talk about doing things differently, like how we spend our money once the kids are out of the house. We try to be sensitive to what the other person is feeling about all these changes. If I were relieved that the kids were out of the house and my husband wasn't, I wouldn't constantly talk about how happy I was if I knew he felt differently. If he were feeling a void, I'd try to suggest things to fill it and find out how I could help him.

When my wife and I met, I was thirty-six years old, working on Wall Street, and it was all about making money. You lose, you make, you lose, you make—that was my life. But what was my purpose? I thought there must be something greater than that. Today my wife and kids give me purpose. I go to work to provide for our family. It gives me a whole new perspective. It simplifies life and brings things into focus. It makes my life easier, not more difficult.

❖

My husband and I have relied on each other financially and emotionally for years. We got together when we were really young, and I know some couples who have gotten together when they're older, and I don't think they're as dependent. I suppose my husband has always looked after me in a way. It's a difficult thing to be so strongly attached. When one of us dies, I don't know how each of us will react to life without the other.

My husband is my best friend and the love of my life. He's gone sometimes for work, and I occasionally need that time to be quiet and left alone. When he's here, though, it's so nice to know that he's at his desk or there if I need something. He's my support, and we're incomplete without the other.

Before I got married in my twenties, I wondered what my wife would look like as an old woman. Would she still be as beautiful? But more than that, would I still be happy that I married her? As we age, it's less about outward and more about inner beauty. I'm getting older, she's getting older. It's wonderful to get older together.

Our bodies eventually all fail, and many of our minds do, too. There's always that fear you could be put out alone on an ice floe. We all have a fear of loneliness, but in marriage, one of you will die first. That's part of the game. I think my husband is thinking he'd like to go before me. Deep down we all have a hope that we'll have somebody to take care of us until death.

As my husband and I get older, we feel more vulnerable, and we feel the other is more vulnerable. We need each other more, not less, as we're getting older. Doors close in your face as you get older. I don't think either one of us could start a new career, for example. We both feel like we've done our thing, and now it's about using creative ways and skills to stay in the workforce, so that's a door that's closed or is closing. As you get older, there are fewer options available. The fact that we have each other is more important today than it was when we were younger.

My husband has said many times that he can't believe he's living with an eighty-five-year-old woman, but the longer we're together, the better it is.

Chapter 12

· ·

COMMITTED

Love seems the swiftest, but it is the slowest of all growths.
No man or woman really knows what perfect love is
until they have been married a quarter of a century.
—Mark Twain

T HIS LAST CHAPTER is all about what it means for couples to be in it
for the long haul. On this subject, the pithy advice often given to
people contemplating marriage is, "Oh, it's a big commitment!"

Commitment. That's a loaded word.

So, once more I wondered, what does "big commitment" really
mean, other than how it's defined as a vow or a promise? And once
people make the commitment, how do they act it out?

How confident are committed couples in the strength and durabil-
ity of their marriages? And decades into the commitment, what does it
feel like?

In answering those questions, I'll leave you with my big three
takeaways from this project, all of which contribute to the meaning of

commitment.

First, the happy couples interviewed for this book didn't talk very much about being in love, but liking each other emerged as a powerful theme. It seems that being "in like," being friends and companions, can be one difference between a dull, vanilla marriage and an interesting, spicy, *happy* one.

This may be because companionship draws people toward each other and reinforces commitment. It strengthens the two people in it. True companions figure each other out and learn what works and what doesn't—and then take action accordingly. They negotiate a life with activities, friends, and goals that meet the needs of both people.

The second revelation about commitment is that happy couples take their marriage seriously. This may sound obvious, but it's not. Marriage for happy couples is an active state of being. It's not just something that happened that one day with the big party and the white dress. It's a present-tense condition that takes daily attention.

Our happy couples know that the relationship always has vulnerabilities. It can get sick and tired. And it can die of neglect.

Marriages are also complex and *changing* year-to-year, week-to-week, sometimes day-to-day. A couple's relationship today isn't the same one it was ten years ago, because the people in it have grown and changed, as has the world around them. A successful marriage will flex and adapt.

The third thing I took away from this project was the realization that as much as marriage is an activity, being committed is also a mindset. For the couples I talked to, being married has become a fundamental part of their individual identities. It's not something they're going to wake up tomorrow and question.

Sure, something unforeseen could happen that might have a negative impact on the marriage. But knowing what they know now, having shared both good times and bad, these couples intend to face the future together, come what may.

In some ways, commitment requires a little faith: looking at the marriage with the belief that it will always be. It will continue to deliver happiness and fun. It will continue to include conflicts and require patience. It will continue to provide comfort and companionship. It will continue to offer safety, intimacy, confidentiality, and a place to call home.

For the happy couples you've spent time with in these pages, the commitment has been made. The marriage is a fact. It's for life, and it's worth all the effort.

Being "in like" is a real thing.

It's important that I like my husband. I might not agree with everything he thinks or does, but it would be impossible to stay together if everything he did annoyed me. It's important to have the love, but if there's no affection and you have nothing in common, then your spouse is just another annoying relative.

I think I could say that I love my children, but I don't always like them. I like my husband all the time.

The number one reason our marriage works is that my wife and I just like being together. We have things to talk about, and we communicate well. The conversation is never dead. There's always something to talk or joke about.

My wife and I have always been good at being bored together. I'm very serious about that. There are a lot of people, people you've dated or people you're friends with, that, as soon as you get bored you just can't stand the sight of each other. When things get really dull, which they do, especially when you have kids, my wife and I can still be completely comfortable around each other. To me, that's a sign that we're best friends.

"Like" is bigger than sex and bigger than money. Everyone thinks it's love, but oh, no. My kids will love me because I'm their mom. My husband will love me as long as his passionate juices are flowing. But that doesn't have anything to do with liking each other. If I feel liked, then I grow and I bloom. Like is the thing that grows the soul.

The idea of liking my wife—that occurs to me all the time after forty years of marriage. We're also intellectual equals. There was a period of time when we were playing Scrabble a lot and keeping a running score. After playing for eighteen months, it was a dead tie. We have friends, of course, but I prefer being with her more than anyone else.

I really look forward to a day out with my husband. So far, in the eight years I've been with him, I've never felt a sick feeling in the pit of my stomach or, even worse, boredom over the idea of doing something with him. We've sometimes been that couple in the restaurant sitting there with nothing to say to each other, and I've thought, *Oh no, we're here. We're over each other.* But mostly it's comfortable silence or, truthfully, we've spent the whole day talking about what we needed to talk about, and we're just done. We spend all our free time together, and I still enjoy his company 100 percent.

Love can be an obligation, and I feel like the word gets overused. What makes our relationship is that I just really like my wife. If you were to ask me, "What do you want to do? You've been working so much." I'd say that I just want to hang out with her. I crave spending more time with her. I don't care what we're doing. I love hanging out with her. I like her outlook on life. I like her physical presence. I like what she has to say. I don't spend as much time worrying about love. I think maybe women do more, but I don't think about that so much. What keeps us together is genuinely liking each other.

I really like my wife. Love is the undercurrent of the whole thing, but I like her. I like to spend time with her, to find out what she's been thinking about. I like to hear from her. And I would say about love, that even though I love her all the time, sometimes I feel it more than others. Sometimes I really am *in love* with her, and I feel it, and I can't wait to get home from work and see her. Sometimes when there's a lot going on, I think that love is the gift in our relationship. I don't have to wonder about that. I don't have to sit around and think, *Do I love her today?* Of course I do. But it helps that I really just like her.

I have these moments sometimes when I'm in a store and my husband is kind enough to look for me, rather than making me meet him at a certain place at a certain time. He'll roam the aisles and find me. I can see him around the corner and totally have that feeling of, *I really like you.* Just the sight of him, he still does it for me that way. It's like a flashback to our past, the early days when we were newly in love. It's a feeling of well-being. I really enjoy his company, and just the sight of him I find very comforting.

Never underestimate the value of a good time. Sometimes you get out of sync with your partner, so for me, when that happens, the best thing is usually to get out of the house and have fun together. That's what got you together in the first place, after all. This isn't to say that we avoid the hard talks or issues, but having fun with my wife reminds me that I like her and that I love her. When you feel that again, then it's easier to deal with the hard stuff.

If you concentrate on the like, the love will work itself out. Love is a pretty heavy thing, and sometimes it's a little too heavy. I think that finding what you like to do with each other, what you like to talk about, what you like to have happen in the house on a regular basis, what you like to have for dinner, sometimes those things go a lot further than focusing on what it means to be in love. And when liking each other is figured out, it makes a lot of room for love to happen naturally.

A good marriage is the ultimate friendship.

My husband and I are friends first and friends last, genuinely each other's best friend. Anything wonderful or horrible that happens, the first person I have to talk to is my husband. The lust and the sex and the kids in between are all important. But if you have kids, they grow up. And then there you are, saying, "Hello, who are you?" At the end of the day, friendship is what makes the marriage work.

I married my best friend, and that's what I tell my girls. My husband is going to be my best friend for the rest of my life.

Being a former divorce attorney, I've heard so many people's stories about how they're not having sex. There's a lot of resentment out there, a lot of dislike. When you feel resentment and you don't like the person you're with, you don't want to have sex with them. You don't want to be vulnerable, and you don't want to be open to them. That's a lot of disconnect.

In our case, the thing that really keeps me interested is that I really like my wife. I love her take on life. I like to hear the way she can get snarky about things. When we're talking, I'm always stimulated. I'm never thinking, *Will you just shut up?* I look at people I know who were in that kind of relationship, and it was like they were embarrassed when their spouse opened their mouth. Not for me. I have a lot of confidence in my wife.

Here's how I judge our success: we'd rather do things with each other over everybody else. We travel well together, for example. If my husband wants to sleep in on vacation, then he sleeps in, and I go out and take pictures. We're relaxed about what we want to do. We've also bought and sold houses four times in the last ten years. I do real estate professionally now and see how couples are awful to each other under the pressure of such a big purchase. Picking the house, how much to spend, how to decorate—all those things are easy hot points for conflict, but we work right through them.

A while back, our son was in a psychology class in which the teacher listed all the things you shouldn't do when you get married—and, of course, the list was everything my wife and I had done. We had a shotgun wedding because she was pregnant, but we defied the odds. There was a lot of luck involved, I think.

There's like and love and lust, and in our case, we had all three going for us at the start. At our age, the lust has pretty much passed on, but the like and the love are still there. You can be in love with somebody you don't particularly like, and that's a prescription for a very difficult marriage. Fortunately, my wife and I like each other. I don't know how you could keep a marriage going for a long time without that.

Liking each other leads to a closeness that helps partners enjoy life more in general. Married life can be more fun than being alone.

It's hard to pinpoint why I like my wife so much. She's someone I like being with and doing things with. I like having a companion, someone to share life with. So much of what I do is more fun when I do it with her.

My wife and I have always kidded each other by saying we're just in "deep like." We love each other, but we also have a lot of fun together.

My husband and I laugh a lot. He's a funny guy, and it's one of the reasons I love him. We have these pictures we had taken where a computer draws you like an artist's sketch. We had them laminated, and they're hilarious, because we're both laughing. They're not very pretty. His mouth is wide open, but they really captured our relationship and who we are.

The reason we're together is because of the bond. I want my wife to be with me because of that. I want her to be happy to see me, happy to talk to me, happy to be with me because she loves me. I don't want her to feel committed, obligated, guilty, or anything other than being with me because she wants to be with me.

Love can have obligation tied to it. Liking is easier, and it's very important. I remember when our kids were young and my husband was out of town on a trip. My sister asked me what I missed most about him when he was gone. I told her that when I got in bed at night, I realized I hadn't had a belly laugh all day long. My husband is so funny. I like a lot of the things he does.

When my husband goes out the door to work in the morning, I don't think, *Finally, I get some time to myself.* I like spending time with him. I find myself thinking throughout the day, *Oh, that's funny, I have to tell him that.* You want to share something pleasurable. Tonight, we get to watch our show on TV together. I like to have those shared experiences. I often think of him when I see something funny. I like it when he laughs.

It can be scary to think about empty nesters, when the kids go away to school and the people look at each other and go, "Who are you?" You had so much going on, and you look at each other and say, "Are we the same? Are we different? We had all these distractions. Did we work on the marriage, or did we only work on taking care of everyone else?"

Maybe that's why marriages after forty or fifty years break up. I don't know, but I wouldn't expect that for my wife and me. We still go out, get in the car, enjoy the same music, and laugh. We'll go to the nicest hotels, like the Ritz Carlton, and bring stuff in. We'll walk in there in sweatpants with our Quiznos and a Big Gulp and get into bed. We're two peas in a pod. That's why I have confidence that this relationship is always going to be.

Growing together doesn't happen naturally. Growing apart is what happens naturally, unless you work to prevent it.

I think you're either growing together or growing apart, and there's very little middle ground. It's scary for my husband and me to think about people who split up. They didn't plan to grow apart, but somehow it happened. We really try to think about what we can do to keep our focus where we want it to be and keep ourselves going down the same path together in life.

Marriage is as hard as they say it will be, and there's no secret formula. Long-term marriages that are successful have their own ingredients that make them work. A chocolate cake may be made with oil, another with butter, and another with mayonnaise. The ingredients are different, but it's still a chocolate cake. Marriage is extremely satisfying and gratifying, but you have to find what works for you, just like everything else in life.

People evolve. You are constantly changing, constantly growing, and you and your partner can go in different directions. It depends what you put your focus on. Let's say I get an opportunity to go to Kenya for a dream job. I'm in love with my work, and I meet a guy who shares my passion. Well, that's it. Then I'm growing in one direction and my husband's growing in another. If I got that opportunity now, I think I'd turn it down. I'm not willing to take that risk.

My wife and I are growing together. I suppose you could grow apart if you were going to insist on your own way, and you can grow apart because your thoughts can be different. You grow together if you learn that it's not that you can't have your own thoughts—you just won't be able to teach your partner to believe exactly the same way you do.

Being married for me means paying attention to your partner, their humor, their state of mind, their health. It's something you're always aware of because they're a part of you. If we ever coasted, it was when our kids were little. It was all about going to work, getting home, taking care of the kids, going to bed, getting up, and doing it again. There was no time that wasn't dedicated to the kids or our jobs, both of which were demanding. We definitely sacrificed our attention to each other for a while, and we had some bumpy times. The marriage always needs tending.

Husbands and wives sometimes take each other for granted, but if you work at it, you can overcome the effects of that. If people allow themselves to become walled in to their own lives and what's happening, they will grow apart. With two separate people in the same house, I'm convinced of that. However, if you truly believe that you are partners trying to deal with the same life events, you'll stretch a little more, even if you don't feel like it. Rather than walling yourself up inside your own silo, you'll try to invest more of yourself in the other person.

Sometimes, when I come home from work, I need to force my wife, a little bit, to give me a kiss. I used to tell her that I didn't care how busy she was, or how tired, that I wanted her to give me a kiss when I got home. I needed to see her smile. She's got the apron on and her sleeves pushed up and she's in the middle of working, but I want acknowledgment that I'm home, and home is happy. There's no reason to do all this work if we don't have that going on. Home is what we're working for.

I don't think there's any formula for who stays together and who breaks up. My husband and I have seen some relationships fall apart that really shocked us when they happened. These were people we thought had a stronger faith than we have, or perhaps came from good families. It's interesting how many times you think people are having this great, wonderful experience, and they're really not. You never know what goes on behind closed doors. My husband and I are committed to being together forever, though, and we're going to continue to work at it.

My husband and I have had married friends who seemed really happy but got divorced. It's been a number of couples we know, not just one. We have a good marriage, but it's important for people to know that happy or good or joyful marriages have their tough moments. I wonder if our friends had those difficult moments but felt like they had to put on this brave face because they thought they were supposed to be happy all the time.

I would say the best marriages have plenty of sadness in them. The presence of sadness and struggle between the two people involved doesn't mean it's not a good marriage or that it doesn't have far more joy and happiness than two lives led individually would have.

Many couples don't view staying together as a choice. It's a decision. Done deal.

I think my husband and I have benefited from the circumstances of our past because our parents are still together on both sides. Anytime the "D-word" is brought up, it's so devastating for both of us to think about. We can't fathom what that would be like. It isn't an option. Part of that is our personalities, too. To us, divorce would be like quitting, and we're not quitters.

They say that in the war of life, you pick the best person to share your foxhole with. My wife and I have done that. We've put all our faith in each other.

I have a lot of confidence in our future together. My wife has more concerns than I do about how we'll interact once the kids are out of the house, because they're such a big part of our lives right now. But I don't. I look at my happiness as being right here in this home. There's nothing I'm looking for beyond this.

My husband is someone who mates for life. I feel like we are rock solid for that reason—not because I don't feel that way, too, but I know that he is super committed. He's not one to hit the road when the going gets tough. Lord knows I've provoked him, and I'm sure he's thought about it once or twice, as I did back in the day. I remember thinking, *Let's cut our losses here*, but we're past that now.

From the start, my wife and I were all in. We knew we were going to survive anything from the start. We both figured that being together was the right path, and we didn't see any reason for that to change.

My wife and I talk about how our lifestyle will change as we get older, but the constant in that picture is being together. It's pretty unthinkable for me not to be with her. I can't imagine finding someone else who'd fill the bill in the same way.

After all the dramas we've had, I can confidently say I love my husband more than I did ten years ago, and even more than yesterday. And I hope I love him more tomorrow than today and that I understand him more as we go. Today, I can say that I'm 100 percent confident that my husband and I are going to stay together.

❖

Ultimately, marriage is a choice. It's something you have to choose each day. Some days, depending on the circumstances, you have to choose it on a minute-by-minute basis. If you don't choose your marriage over another person or a job or a hobby or a habit, it will impact the relationship. Maybe not at first, but I've seen those seeds grow into weeds that can crack a sidewalk.

❖

I think, at a certain point, you don't overthink the commitment. I don't get it when people are coming up with these long lists of grievances, the gist of which has to do with the heart of the marriage and whether it will continue. I mean, you're married.

Years ago, I was traveling with a couple of guys I worked with. One was twice divorced and looking forward to meeting up with a girl he'd met at a swinger's club. The other guy was Korean, and he was about to go back home to meet the wife that his parents had chosen for him as an arranged marriage.

The three of us were talking in the airport, and we were asking the Korean guy about the arranged marriage because it seemed so archaic to us. The other guy was really making fun of him, scoffing at the idea that anyone would ever marry for anything but true love.

Now, it's ten years later, and the guy in the arranged marriage is still married, and the "true love" guy just finalized his third divorce. If you're relying on love to carry you through, you're probably not going to make it. I think success for my wife and me is not just a willingness to put effort into our marriage but also an investment, right from the start, that this is how it's going to be.

When I think back to when I was single years ago, I've changed my mindset. I now think of myself first as a member of a couple and then as a member of a family. If I analyze myself right, it's how I unconsciously think of myself now—not as an individual by myself, out for myself.

I have confidence that my wife and I will be together for the rest of our days, because I love her and want to be with her. I'll do everything in my power to make sure that happens. I can't imagine another scenario for us.

I've never heard a wedding vow that said, "I'm going to love, honor, and cherish you for the next two years." Do people actually stand there at the altar and say the words while they're really thinking, *I'm just going to do this for a while, as long as it feels good*? You made a vow. And now this goes to your own upbringing and values: How important is a vow? There are people who stand by their word, and there are people who don't. Sometimes people break that vow intentionally, and sometimes inadvertently. But when you talk about forever, you need to think, *Is it really forever*? For my wife and me, it was an unqualified forever.

In a marriage, you learn how to live together and how to appreciate each other. Pretty soon, you learn to predict what the other person's reaction will be in situations, or at least pretty close. You each have different talents, you have different backgrounds, and that begins to meld together over time. For some people, traumatic things might happen that would split them up. But under normal circumstances, I think you need to say, "This is who I'm going to be with for the rest of my life."

It's important early in marriage to make the decision that you're going to stay together no matter what. After you get married, you may have those thoughts like, *Did I make the right decision? Did I choose the right person? Is this person the same one I thought she was?* I think it's necessary in tough times that you try to make changes, because the alternative just isn't worth it.

It's a good thing, and a helpful thing, to know that my wife and I are absolutely committed to staying together. We believe that the marriage is going to work and going to continue. It's a very strange thing, and horrifying to me, to think about long-running emotional roller coasters about whether two people's marriage is going to continue. For me, it's absolutely a nonissue. It's off the table. Someone once asked Ruth Graham, Billy Graham's wife, about whether she ever thought about divorce. And she smiled and said, "Divorce, no. Murder, yes." And I like that. I like the sentiment.

Just because it's work doesn't mean it's not enjoyable. That's the negative connotation of working at the relationship, but that's sometimes the best part.

I think of happiness as a sort of transitory, fleeting feeling. Over the long term our marriage has given us much happiness, but it's not because we seek out happiness, and certainly not in the moment. I think we seek out integrity and truth and a commitment to good things ahead of seeking out happiness. I'd trade companionship or long-term joy for happiness, and I think my wife and I do in our marriage.

My wife and I are very happy at times, but we also have our struggles. I don't think we have the easiest marriage. We've met people who have been married for far longer than we have and legitimately don't fight about anything. They're just very much in step with each other. My wife and I, by nature, are not. We are critical of ourselves, and we're critical of each other. In the long term, we value that. We're edified by it, actually, even though in the short term it can be difficult.

I'd never had a lot of stability in my life. Most of the people I work with are single, and it reminds me of when I was single. I see them going out for happy hour, and I'm sure some of them are having fun, but I know that I have something more relaxing to go home to now. I look forward to seeing my wife at the end of the day. I know that what I'm driving home to is rock solid.

ACKNOWLEDGMENTS

This book exists entirely because of the generosity of the happy couples who agreed to be interviewed. I'm in their debt, not just for the time and thought they put into our interviews, but for their openness in discussing delicate, painful, and difficult things. I thank them for their trust.

I'm also grateful to friends, family, and colleagues who agreed to read early drafts of this book and so thoughtfully gave feedback of both the positive and negative variety. The book is better for it.

Thanks to Patrick Price, editor and fun guy to talk to, for the feedback and input on making this work clear and readable. Thanks also to Kaitlin Carruthers-Busser for sweating the details in copyediting and to Michael Rehder for the kickass cover design.

After writing this book, I have renewed gratitude to my parents, Don and Helen, who are gone but showed me and my siblings what a happy marriage was from the beginning. For forty-six years, it wasn't all laughs, but there were plenty of them—as well as faith, forgiveness, patience, generosity, and many of the other virtues highlighted in this book. Good models, indeed.

Finally, I want to acknowledge my husband, Barry Rinehart, the love of my life. He always believes in what I create and encouraged me to write this book from the start. I am so grateful to be with someone who makes it easier when times are tough, and even sweeter when they're good.

ABOUT THE AUTHOR

CLAIRE VANDE POLDER is a nonfiction television producer and writer. She began her career at National Geographic Television in Washington, DC. After traveling the world, she joined the Discovery Health Channel as an executive producer. Since then she has worked independently with a variety of networks and production companies such as TLC, ID (Investigation Discovery), Smithsonian Channel, HGTV, Oprah Winfrey's Harpo Studios, and others. She has a B.A. in English from Calvin College and an M.A. in 19th Century English and American Literature from King's College London. She lives with her husband in South Florida.

CONNECT WITH CLAIRE

Claire can be reached via her author website, ClaireVandePolder.com, where you can give feedback and check out what she's writing next.

If you have a great story about marriage, or some life wisdom worth sharing, she'd love to hear from you.

And for book groups, head over to the website for a free set of discussion questions.

Finally, do you want to help out an indie author?

Other than recommending this book to your friends, the most helpful thing you can do is to **leave a review online**. Please consider posting a review for *Making Marriage Happy* on Amazon, or wherever you bought this book. It doesn't need to be long to be helpful.

Thank you!

Made in the USA
Monee, IL
16 February 2021

60657718R00135